T0308939

The WEEKNIGHT Cookbook

For my precious triplet nieces,
Mabel, Nora and Poppy. You've only
just turned one, but I am very much looking
forward to you cooking for me in my old age!

The WEEKNIGHT *Cookbook*

Create 100+ delicious new meals
using pantry staples

Justine Schofield

CONTENTS

INTRODUCTION

I am tirelessly curious about pantries, freezers and fridges. Over the years, I've popped my head into pantries in France, Italy, America, Japan and, of course, Australia. I've spied oodles of oddly shaped pasta, canisters of pulses and thousands of grains, and pondered just how many types of pickles are reasonable (23 jars in my pantry at last count!). I've sifted through rows of stacked spices and been delighted by memorable discoveries, such as bottarga, gochujang, Chinese black vinegar, preserved seafood and pots of terrines and pâtés.

Fridges and freezers receive the same nosy-parker treatment. On any given visit to my parents' or closest friends' homes, you'll find me sorting through their fridges, sniffing leftovers and uncovering the most unlikely treasures. Who knew leftover meatloaf and spicy celery pickles could be quite so delicious sandwiched between two slices of buttered white bread?

These little trips to the nerve centre of the kitchen – pantry, fridge, freezer – reveal so much about their human moderators. Some are meticulously organised, others are heaving with produce, and some of my favourites look like the ultimate foodies' bazaar. I like to think of my own as a quick map of places visited. On my travels I've collected so many preserved foods – they're just so handy and add value to so many dishes. A chutney from a local school fête, delectable pickled turnips my friend Pedro made from scratch, and tuna fillets in oil prepared by my Uncle Thierry after he was lucky enough to catch a big fish are just a few. Nothing goes to waste, and the homemade taste is always superior.

I grew up in a family with two working parents. Saturday was always shopping day at the supermarket, greengrocer, fishmonger, butcher, deli and, occasionally, the markets, and our weeknight dinners were fast. Each week by Friday, my brothers and I complained about the empty fridge, but it was not empty to my parents' keen eyes. They whipped up kitchen creations like lentils and sausages (page 137), meatloaf (page 108) or bread-and-butter pudding (page 191). Mum, in particular, showed me that even a basic omelette makes a delicious meal in minutes when teamed with a quick green salad and a splash of vinegar and olive oil. Her innovation transformed seemingly simple ingredients, teaching me the value of not wasting a thing and how to be nifty with a handful of standby staples and leftovers.

So, let's talk staples. Never underestimate the power of a well-stocked pantry. It will not only save you money in the long run, but will allow you to whip up magical creations with humble ingredients, such as dried lentils, peas, canned tomatoes, peanut butter, breadcrumbs, noodles, rice or canned beans. You'll find lots of ideas in this book for using these inexpensive kitchen essentials. And an assortment of vinegars, Asian sauces, nut milks, mustards and chilli pastes have the ability to give everyday raw ingredients the flavour-bomb effect.

The same rule applies to the fridge. My obsession with cheese means I have a whole section in my fridge dedicated to a variety of dairy products, particularly the ever-versatile ricotta and parmesan, along with cheddar and a little camembert – my Achilles heel! If you don't already have it in your fridge, miso is something I hope you will embrace. Its umami flavour profile value-adds to so many dishes: sauces, dressings, soups, stews and quick marinades (to make salmon shine, see my Crispy Salmon with Japanese 'Pantry Sauce' on page 98). The French part of me also ensures I always have cream, butter and treasured eggs, as there are countless ways to use them.

This brings me to the freezer: stock it well and weeknight dinners will always be a breeze. Not just with the basics, such as peas, spinach, pastry, stocks, mince, chicken and sausages, but also leftovers. Make big batches of chilli con carne, chicken stew, meatballs, curries and dumplings, and freeze some. If you store them correctly, you'll have a steady supply of meals, and also bases to invent new dishes, for months to come. For example, the chicken stew from the Chicken and Mushroom Cottage Pie on page 168 can be transformed into pot pies or party pies or simply tossed with pasta. Another creative – and clever – little trick is to freeze any leftover wine that has been opened. Decant into zip-lock bags and freeze. It's great to have on standby when making risottos, stews and sauces.

Most importantly, waste not, want not. Most of the recipes you'll find in this book are created using kitchen staples, supplemented with a few fresh ingredients to pack a serious palate punch. With correct storage, the shelf life of fresh herbs, fruits and vegetables is greatly increased. Place herbs in damp paper towel and then wrap in plastic. In France, many households have a salad bag – a perfect crisper-sized, zipped, fabric pouch to store lettuce. You can purchase these from specialty grocers or simply make your own by using a recycled plastic bag and lining it with damp paper towel. This storage method doubles or even triples the lifetime of your lettuce leaves, saving you shopping time and money. Pickles, kimchi and jams come in handy re-usable glass jars, so don't throw them away. They are perfect to store your dried fruit, seeds and nuts.

If you do substitute ingredients when cooking, be sure to jot down your notes and personal tweaks. I don't want you to be precious with these recipes. I want them to evolve into your own, which will help you create memorable weeknight dinners. Don't be afraid to tinker and substitute seasonal ingredients or pantry supplies you have on hand. For example, if you don't have olives, you can achieve a pop of saltiness with capers. If you don't have black vinegar, use balsamic – it works surprisingly well. Cookbooks shouldn't be pristine. The most loved and often-used ones are always particularly well thumbed, with splattered stains and greasy marks from poring over the recipes. Alongside your personal notes, this creates a handy notebook of recipes that work for you and your household.

And don't forget – many hands make light work. Over the years, I've had friends around for countless weeknight dinners and every time, without fail, people offer to help. Give them jobs, big and small, such as spinning lettuce leaves, chopping tomatoes or making fresh breadcrumbs with stale bread. Busy, nimble fingers are excellent for creating yummy morsels to bulk out weeknight dinners and complete them even faster. There's nothing I like more than having my loved ones with me in my kitchen, helping to create a meal. I know these will always be the tastiest and most memorable ones.

At the end of the day, I want you to enjoy weeknight cooking more and feel empowered in the kitchen. Even with our busy schedules, it shouldn't be a chore, and that's why this book follows my working-week mantra: work smarter, not harder. I've collated these scrumptious and speedy recipes to give you more time to savour sharing the food you prepare; after all, the joy in cooking is sharing meals with your friends and family. So, dip into your well stocked pantry and freezer, and add plenty of seasonal fruit and vegetables from the fridge. You'll be surprised how quickly your repertoire expands and just how easy it is to make fresh home-cooked dinners every night of the week.

PANTRY STAPLES

The following lists are my essential pantry staples – the building blocks for all of the meals in this book.
Poke your nose into my fridge, freezer and pantry on any given day and this is what you will find!

FREEZER

Baby peas
Spinach

Filo pastry
Puff pastry
Shortcrust pastry

Flour tortillas
Pita bread

Mince
Sausages

FRIDGE

Butter
Cheddar
Cream
Feta
Milk
Parmesan
Ricotta
Sour cream
Yoghurt

Chilli paste
Dijon mustard
Harissa paste
Hot English mustard
Mayonnaise
Miso paste
Tomato paste

Oyster sauce
Tabasco sauce
Tomato relish
Tomato sauce

Leftover cooked rice

Anchovies
Bacon
Chorizo sausage

Carrots

Capers
Gherkins
Jarred roasted capsicum
Kimchi
Marinated artichoke hearts
Pickles

Eggs
Silken tofu

PANTRY

Apples
French shallots
Fresh ginger
Garlic
Lemons
Onions
Potatoes
Red onions
Sweet potatoes

Almond meal
Almonds
Cashews
Flaked almonds
Hazelnuts
Nut meal
Peanuts
Pine nuts
Pistachios
Walnuts

Dates
Dried apricots
Flaked coconut
Prunes
Raisins

Canned chickpeas
Canned kidney beans
Canned lentils
Canned pineapple slices
Canned salmon
Canned tuna in oil
Canned tuna in spring
    water
Canned white beans
Canned whole peeled
    tomatoes
Coconut cream
Tomato passata

Dried brown lentils
Dried chickpeas
Dried porcini mushrooms
Dried puy lentils
Dried yellow split peas

Apple cider vinegar
Balsamic vinegar
Black vinegar
Rice wine vinegar

Sherry vinegar
White wine vinegar

Fish sauce
Hoisin sauce
Kecap manis
Light soy sauce
Soy sauce
Stock
Worcestershire sauce

Madras curry paste
Red curry paste
Sambal oelek
Tahini
Tomato paste

Honey
Jam
Peanut butter

Coconut oil
Grapeseed oil
Olive oil
Peanut oil
Sesame oil
Vegetable oil

Brandy
Coffee liqueur
Dark rum
Marsala
Port
Sake
Shaoxing wine
Sherry
White wine

Couscous
Crispy fried shallots
Hokkien noodles
Pasta
Quinoa
Rice
Soba noodles
Vermicelli
Wonton wrappers

Bread
Pita bread
Fresh breadcrumbs
Panko breadcrumbs

Brown sugar
Caster sugar
Cocoa powder
Coffee
Cornflour
Dark chocolate
Gelatine leaves
Icing sugar
Instant yeast
Plain flour
Quick oats
Self-raising flour
Sugar

SPICE RACK

Bay leaves
Black pepper
Black sesame seeds
Cardamom pods
Cayenne pepper
Chilli flakes
Chilli powder
Chinese five spice
Cinnamon sticks
Cloves
Coriander seeds
Cumin seeds
Curry leaves
Curry powder
Dried mint
Dried oregano
Green peppercorns
Ground allspice
Ground cinnamon
Ground cloves
Ground coriander
Ground cumin
Ground ginger
Ground turmeric
Nutmeg
Ras el hanout
Saffron
Salt
Sesame seeds
Smoked paprika
Star anise
Sumac
Vanilla extract
Vanilla pods

VEGETABLES

ROASTED BROCCOLINI SALAD WITH BAKED RICOTTA

Broccolini lends itself nicely to cheese and takes on a more intense flavour when roasted. The ricotta component here really makes this dish shine: when baked, the creamy, fluffy texture of the cheese becomes firmer and crumblier and has a lovely salty flavour, which perfectly matches the sweet broccolini, the zingy balsamic and the herbaceous dried mint.

SERVES: 4   PREP: 15 MINUTES, PLUS 30 MINUTES DRAINING TIME (OPTIONAL)
COOK: 40 MINUTES

1 x 500 g fresh, full-fat ricotta wedge ('basket' ricotta, not the smooth variety sold in a tub)
3 tablespoons olive oil, plus extra for drizzling
salt flakes
pinch of dried mint
50 g unsalted pistachio kernels
3 bunches of broccolini (about 600 g), trimmed
freshly ground black pepper
1 garlic clove, finely chopped
1 tablespoon balsamic vinegar
4 dates, pitted and finely chopped

If the ricotta is a little wet, place it in a colander lined with muslin or a new Chux cloth and set aside to drain for 30 minutes. Pat dry.

Preheat the oven to 180°C. Drizzle a little oil on a baking tray.

Place the wedge of ricotta on the prepared tray, drizzle on some more oil and season with a pinch of salt and the dried mint. Bake for 20–30 minutes until the ricotta is starting to colour. Add the pistachios to one side of the tray and return to the oven for 10 minutes until the ricotta is golden and the pistachios are toasted.

Meanwhile, prepare the broccolini. Cut any larger stems in half lengthways; keep the thinner ones intact. Place in a baking dish and drizzle with a little oil. Season with salt and pepper and roast for 12–15 minutes (you can do this while the ricotta is in the oven) until the broccolini is slightly coloured but still a little crisp.

Place the garlic, balsamic, 3 tablespoons of oil and a pinch of salt and pepper in a small bowl and whisk to form a dressing. Stir through the chopped dates.

While the broccolini is still hot, pour over the dressing; toss and place on a platter. Roughly chop the toasted pistachios. Crumble the baked ricotta over the broccolini and sprinkle over the pistachios.

PANTRY STAPLES
Balsamic vinegar
Dates
Dried mint
Garlic
Olive oil
Pistachio kernels
Ricotta
Salt and pepper

SHOPPING LIST
Broccolini

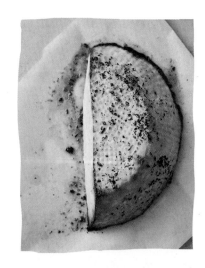

BABA GANOUSH AND FLATBREAD

Once eggplant has been cooked, the flesh completely transforms and becomes creamy and earthy. Baba ganoush is one of the most famous dishes to create with this versatile nightshade vegetable. Serve your smoky puree with simple flatbreads, for the perfect entertaining starter. Some cooks like to use the juices that gather in the bowl while the eggplant cools, but I find them bitter, so I don't add them.

SERVES: 4   PREP: 30 MINUTES, PLUS 1 HOUR 20 MINUTES STANDING
AND PROVING   COOK: 30 MINUTES

100 ml warm water
2 teaspoons (7 g sachet)
   dried instant yeast
1 teaspoon caster sugar
150 g (1 cup) plain flour,
   plus extra for dusting
salt flakes
olive oil, for brushing

BABA GANOUSH
2 large eggplants
2 tablespoons hulled tahini
½ garlic clove, grated
juice of ½ lemon, plus extra to serve
3 tablespoons extra-virgin olive oil,
   plus extra to serve
salt flakes and freshly ground
   black pepper
1 large handful of flat-leaf
   parsley leaves
50 g (⅓ cup) whole almonds,
   toasted

PANTRY STAPLES   **SHOPPING LIST**
Almonds   Eggplant
Caster sugar   Fresh flat-leaf
Extra-virgin olive oil   parsley
Garlic
Hulled tahini
Instant yeast
Lemon
Plain flour
Salt and pepper

Place the warm water, yeast, sugar and a pinch of flour in a small bowl and set aside in a warm spot to activate. It will take 15–20 minutes to become foamy (active).

Mix the remaining flour and a pinch of salt in a bowl, then pour in the activated yeast mixture and combine with a wooden spoon until a sticky dough forms. Turn out onto a lightly floured work surface and knead the dough for 3–4 minutes. Sprinkle a little extra flour into the bowl and return the dough. Cover with plastic wrap and set aside to prove in a warm spot for 30–60 minutes until doubled in size.

Remove the dough from the bowl and knead again on a floured surface for a minute until smooth and elastic. Cut the dough into four equal portions and roll out each piece into 1 cm thick rounds. Place a sheet of baking paper between each flatbread and cover with a clean tea towel until ready to cook.

Meanwhile, to make the baba ganoush, place the eggplants directly on the open flame of a gas hob and char, turning occasionally, for 10–15 minutes until mostly blackened and soft. If you don't have a gas burner, preheat the grill element in the oven, place the eggplants on a baking tray and grill, turning regularly; alternatively, chargrill on the barbecue. Place the charred eggplants in a colander over a bowl and cover with plastic wrap. Cool for 15–20 minutes and allow the juices to drain. When cool enough to handle, carefully peel away the blackened skin and discard the juices. Place the eggplant flesh in a bowl, add the tahini, garlic, lemon juice and oil, season to taste with salt and pepper and, using a fork, mash until a rough puree forms.

Transfer the baba ganoush to a serving dish. Dress the parsley leaves with a little extra lemon juice and oil, scatter over the baba ganoush, then sprinkle on the almonds.

Heat a chargrill pan over high heat or a barbecue to hot and grill the flatbreads, one or two at a time, for 1 minute on each side until puffed and charred. Brush with some extra olive oil while still hot and serve immediately with the baba ganoush.

BRUSSELS SPROUT SLAW

*I had this salad in a restaurant in Los Angeles, and it completely transformed the way
I prepare brussels sprouts. Gone are the days of boiling these baby cabbages to death;
now it's all about roasting, grilling or even eating them raw, as in this recipe. The key
here is to shred them as finely as you can, which gives the slaw a more refined flavour
as the dressing is better able to coat the sprouts.*

SERVES: 4–6 PREP: 20 MINUTES, PLUS 10 MINUTES STANDING TIME COOK: 10 MINUTES

80 g (½ cup) whole almonds
80 g parmesan
500 g brussels sprouts
salt flakes
3 tablespoons sherry vinegar
80 ml (⅓ cup) olive oil
freshly ground black pepper
200 g seedless red grapes, halved

Preheat the oven to 180°C.

Place the almonds on a baking tray and roast in the oven for
8–10 minutes, tossing halfway through, until golden brown.
Set aside to cool.

Roughly chop the parmesan, place in a food processor and pulse
four or five times to make a fine crumb. Tip out into a bowl.
Alternatively, you can finely grate the cheese.

Place the thin slicing attachment in the food processor and feed the
brussels sprouts through the shoot until they are evenly shredded.
Alternatively, finely shred with a sharp knife or a mandoline. The
aim is to slice the brussels sprouts as thinly as possible.

Place the shredded sprouts in a large bowl and add ¼ teaspoon of
salt. Use your hands to scrunch the salt into the sprouts, then stand
for 10 minutes to soften and tenderise.

Whisk together the sherry vinegar, oil, a pinch of pepper and
one-third of the parmesan in a bowl.

Pour the dressing over the brussels sprouts and toss through the
grapes, almonds and the remaining parmesan. Pile up in a shallow
bowl and serve.

PANTRY STAPLES
Almonds
Olive oil
Parmesan
Salt and pepper
Sherry vinegar

SHOPPING LIST
Brussels sprouts
Red grapes

CACIO E PEPE PUMPKIN

Cacio e pepe, meaning 'cheese and pepper' in Italian, is usually associated with the famous Roman pasta dish. Here, I use this simple combination to make pumpkin shine. I originally prepared this recipe using parmesan on my show Everyday Gourmet, *but I think the sweetness of the pumpkin and the heat from the pepper are even better paired with blue cheese. Serve with roast chicken or lamb chops, or toss with crisp lettuce leaves for a warm salad.*

SERVES: 4   PREP: 10 MINUTES   COOK: 35 MINUTES

1 tablespoon black peppercorns
3 tablespoons extra-virgin olive oil
salt flakes
½ kent pumpkin, cut into wedges
100 g blue cheese (such as Danish
    blue or gorgonzola)

PANTRY STAPLES
Black peppercorns
Extra-virgin olive oil
Salt

SHOPPING LIST
Blue cheese
Kent pumpkin

Preheat the oven to 180°C. Line a baking tray with baking paper.

Crush the peppercorns using a mortar and pestle, drizzle in the oil and mix to form a paste. Season with salt, then drizzle over the pumpkin and rub in. Place the pumpkin on the prepared tray and bake for 30–35 minutes until just tender.

Crumble the blue cheese over the top and serve.

* The cheese is interchangeable; this recipe also works really well with pecorino, parmesan or feta.

PICKLED CELERY

Pickling is a great way to preserve an overabundance of vegetables, and I always seem to have too much celery on hand. Pickling keeps it lovely and crisp and the chilli and classic spices add a great punch. It's best to leave the celery to pickle for a few hours to allow it to take on all the lovely flavours. Pickled celery is a wonderful addition to any cheese board, antipasto platter or salad, or even as a side for roast chicken.

MAKES: 1 × 1 LITRE JAR **PREP:** 10 MINUTES, PLUS AT LEAST
2 HOURS PICKLING **COOK:** 2 MINUTES

5 celery stalks, trimmed
2 teaspoons coriander seeds
½ teaspoon black peppercorns
1 cinnamon stick
2 fresh bay leaves
375 ml (1½ cups) apple cider vinegar
220 g (1 cup) sugar
2 teaspoons salt flakes
1 small onion, finely sliced
1 long green chilli, sliced on an
   angle into 1 cm lengths

On the grooved side of the celery stalks, cut halfway through the wider end and pull away the stringy, fibrous strands. Cut on an angle into 1 cm lengths.

Place the spices and bay leaves in a saucepan along with the vinegar, sugar and salt. Bring to the boil and stir to dissolve the sugar. Remove from the heat.

Place the celery, onion and chilli in a sterilised 1 litre preserving jar (see Note) and pour over the hot pickling liquid, spices and bay leaves. Seal tightly and set aside to cool to room temperature. Transfer to the fridge. The celery can be eaten straight away, but keeps for up to 3 months in the fridge, and as the weeks go on the taste improves.

PANTRY STAPLES
Apple cider vinegar
Black peppercorns
Cinnamon stick
Coriander seeds
Onion
Salt
Sugar

SHOPPING LIST
Celery
Fresh bay leaves
Fresh long green
   chilli

* To prevent mould and bacteria forming, and to give your pickles a longer shelf life, it is essential to sterilise your jars. Preheat the oven to 120°C, place the washed glass jars and lids (not plastic) on a baking tray and heat in the oven for 20 minutes. Fill the still-hot jars immediately.

This pickling method works really well with other vegetables, such as turnip, carrot, fennel and cucumber.

CAULIFLOWER AND CAMEMBERT CHEESE

*I love the traditional way of making cauliflower cheese, but I've given this nostalgic dish
a modern twist by roasting the cauliflower until it's sweet and nutty and teaming it with my
favourite cheese, camembert. This recipe is so delicious and you can decide how much you
want to show off the pungent cheese. For a milder flavour, use a young cheese or
even a brie; for a big, bold version, get a more mature camembert.*

SERVES: 4   PREP: 15 MINUTES   COOK: 35 MINUTES

1 large head of cauliflower
    (about 1.5 kg)
1 tablespoon olive oil, plus extra
    for shallow-frying
salt flakes and freshly ground
    black pepper
400 ml milk
200 g camembert, rind removed,
    cut into chunks
12 sage leaves
50 g (½ cup) walnuts, toasted

Preheat the oven to 180°C. Line a large baking tray with
baking paper.

Cut the cauliflower into eight equal wedges, making sure
to include the stem so the wedges stay intact. Finely chop two
of the wedges and place in a saucepan. Arrange the remaining
wedges on the prepared tray in one layer, drizzle over 1 tablespoon
of oil and season with salt and pepper. Roast for 30–35 minutes,
turning halfway through, until golden brown and just tender with
a slight crunch.

While the cauliflower is roasting, make the sauce by adding the
milk to the pan of finely chopped cauliflower. Season with a small
pinch of salt and bring to the boil. Cook for 10–12 minutes until
the cauliflower is soft. Drain the cauliflower (reserve the milk
for another use – I like to add it to creamy soups) and place in
a blender. Add the camembert and blend to form a smooth and
silky puree.

Heat some oil in a small saucepan over medium heat, add the sage
leaves and cook for 3–4 seconds until just crisp. Remove and drain
on paper towel.

Spread the sauce over the base of a shallow dish, pile the roasted
cauliflower on top and scatter over the walnuts and sage leaves.

PANTRY STAPLES   **SHOPPING LIST**

Milk   Camembert
Olive oil   Cauliflower
Salt and pepper   Fresh sage
Walnuts

JAPANESE CABBAGE SALAD

Miso paste is an instant flavour bomb we should all have in our fridge. Because of its complex umami flavour profile, it's incredibly versatile. Here, I've used it in a quick dressing to create a scrumptious cabbage salad. There are many varieties of miso available: from dark (salty and earthy) to white (sweet and fruity). Add a little less for this dressing if using a darker variety. Find it in the Asian aisle of your supermarket, at Asian grocers or at health-food stores.

SERVES: 4   PREP: 20 MINUTES

¼ white cabbage (about 300 g), finely shredded (I like to do this on a mandoline)
1 carrot, julienned
3 tablespoons crispy fried shallots
1 tablespoon black sesame seeds

DRESSING
1 tablespoon white (shiro) miso paste
2 cm piece of ginger, finely chopped
1 tablespoon honey
1 tablespoon rice wine vinegar
1 tablespoon sesame oil
2 tablespoons grapeseed or vegetable oil

To make the dressing, whisk all the ingredients together in a bowl until smooth.

Place the cabbage and carrot in a bowl and toss well. Pour on the dressing and mix everything with your hands. It's okay to bruise the cabbage a bit as this helps to tenderise it.

Transfer the salad to a shallow dish and top with the fried shallots and sesame seeds.

PANTRY STAPLES
Black sesame seeds
Carrots
Crispy fried shallots
Fresh ginger
Grapeseed or vegetable oil
Honey
Rice wine vinegar
Sesame oil
White miso paste

SHOPPING LIST
White cabbage

SUPER-CRUNCHY ROAST POTATOES

I am often asked how I make roast potatoes, so it is only appropriate that I include my recipe here. I don't like to add garlic or herbs, as they tend to burn. Instead, I let the potatoes shine in all their glory and focus on achieving the crispiest result. The key points are to give yourself a bit of time to dry out the potatoes – moisture is the enemy here – and to get the oil nice and hot to create a preliminary crust, which will become even crunchier by the end of the cooking process, leaving a fluffy interior.

SERVES: 4–6   PREP: 15 MINUTES, PLUS 1 HOUR 10 MINUTES COOLING
COOK: 1 HOUR 20 MINUTES

2 kg sebago potatoes (or king edwards or any other floury potato, often called 'brushed potatoes' in the supermarket), peeled and washed well
salt flakes
3 tablespoons vegetable oil

Place the potatoes in a large saucepan and cover with plenty of cold water. Add a pinch of salt and bring to the boil. Once boiling, cook for 15–20 minutes until the potatoes are just tender when pierced with a skewer. Drain and shake the potatoes in the colander to roughen the edges. (The rougher the edges the better, as this gives the potatoes a crispier result.) It's okay, even desirable, if they break up. Break any remaining whole potatoes in half with the tip of a knife (almost as if you were cracking the potato in two to create a jagged edge) and place on a wire rack. Place the smaller broken-up potatoes on the rack as well and leave for 8–10 minutes until the steam has dissipated. Transfer the rack to the fridge to allow the potato pieces to air-dry for 1 hour (you can do this step a day ahead).

Preheat the oven to 180°C and remove the potato from the fridge.

Place the oil in a roasting tin and heat in the oven for 5–8 minutes. Carefully remove the tin from the oven and add the potato. Using a spatula, gently turn the potato in the hot oil to evenly coat. Season with salt. Roast for 50–60 minutes, tossing two or three times to ensure all sides are crunchy and golden brown. Season again before serving if required.

PANTRY STAPLES   **SHOPPING LIST**
Potatoes
Salt
Vegetable oil

SPINACH GRATIN

*This is my take on the old-fashioned creamed spinach. I love turning it into
a decadent gratin that is made even more delicious with the addition of béchamel.
This is the perfect side to roast chicken or fish.*

SERVES: 4–6   PREP: 15 MINUTES   COOK: 50 MINUTES

1.5 kg English spinach
   (4–5 bunches)
2 teaspoons olive oil
20 g butter
1 onion, finely chopped
250 ml (1 cup) thickened cream
2 tablespoons dijon mustard
pinch of cayenne pepper, plus extra
   for sprinkling
½ teaspoon freshly grated nutmeg
salt flakes
80 g Gruyère cheese,
   coarsely grated
50 g panko breadcrumbs

Cut 6 cm off the spinach stalks – it's okay if there is some stalk left.
Wash the spinach very well, then drain.

Bring a large saucepan of salted water to the boil. Add the spinach,
a handful at a time, so it all fits in the pan. Bring back to the boil
and cook for 1 minute. Drain in a colander and set aside to cool.
When the spinach is cool enough to handle, squeeze out as much
water as possible.

Preheat the oven to 200°C.

Heat 1 teaspoon of the oil and the butter in a saucepan over medium
heat. Add the onion and cook for 5–8 minutes until softened with
no colour. Add the cream and bring to the boil, then simmer, stirring
frequently, until thick and reduced by a third. Stir in the mustard and
cook for a further 1 minute. Remove from the heat, season with the
cayenne pepper, nutmeg and a pinch of salt and add half the cheese.

Add the spinach to the cream sauce and fold through.

Mix the remaining cheese with the breadcrumbs and use your
hands to rub in the remaining oil.

Spread the spinach mixture evenly into a 1.5 litre gratin dish.
Top with the breadcrumb mixture and an extra pinch of cayenne
and bake for 20–25 minutes until the top is golden brown.

* You can substitute fresh spinach with three 250 g portions of
frozen spinach, or change the spinach for other leafy greens, such
as silverbeet, Swiss chard or kale, or even cabbage. The kale and
cabbage need to be boiled for longer (5–6 minutes), as they're
a hardier leaf.

You could also use cheddar instead of Gruyère cheese, if you like.

PANTRY STAPLES   **SHOPPING LIST**
Butter   English spinach
Cayenne pepper   Gruyère cheese
Dijon mustard
Nutmeg
Olive oil
Onion
Panko breadcrumbs
Salt
Thickened cream

SIMPLE SALADS & SIDES

1. For a healthy dip for crudité vegetables and crackers, soak 155 g (1 cup) of raw cashews in 250 ml (1 cup) of boiling water for 20 minutes. Drain, reserving 125 ml (½ cup) of liquid. Place the nuts in a blender. Add a pinch of salt and pepper, ½ garlic clove, a small handful each of basil and flat-leaf parsley leaves, 1 tablespoon of olive oil and the reserved water. Blend until smooth.

2. Wrap long strips of streaky bacon around baby new potatoes and fasten with toothpicks. Place on a baking tray on a bed of rosemary and thyme. Coat everything in olive oil and season with a small pinch of salt. Roast at 180°C for 30–40 minutes.

3. Roast 2 eggplants at 200°C for 45 minutes until very soft. Cover and set aside to cool. Discard the skin and slice the flesh. Combine 1 tablespoon of white (shiro) miso paste, 1 tablespoon each of rice wine vinegar, soy sauce and honey, 1 teaspoon of sesame oil and 2 tablespoons of grapeseed or vegetable oil in a bowl. Whisk and drizzle over the eggplant. Scatter on some toasted sesame seeds.

4. For baked rice, fry 1 chopped onion in a tablespoon of oil in an ovenproof sauté pan. Add a thyme sprig and 400 g (2 cups) of rinsed long-grain rice. Coat in the onion mixture and season with a pinch of salt. Cover with 800 ml of chicken stock or enough to cover the rice by 3 cm. Bring to the boil and cover. Bake at 180°C for 20–25 minutes.

5. Char quartered pears and sliced haloumi in a chargrill pan or on a barbecue. Arrange on a platter of radicchio or rocket leaves. Dress with balsamic vinegar and olive oil and scatter over toasted walnuts.

6. Halve a butternut pumpkin lengthways, drizzle over olive oil and season. Bake at 200°C for 45 minutes until tender. Mix 185 g (¾ cup) of Greek yoghurt, 1 finely chopped garlic clove, 1 teaspoon of maple syrup and ½ teaspoon each of ground cumin, smoked paprika and grated lemon zest in a bowl. Drizzle over the hot pumpkin, then scatter on some flat-leaf parsley leaves and pumpkin seeds.

7. Finely slice ½ red onion and place in a bowl. Add a good pinch of salt and 1 tablespoon of white wine vinegar. Set aside to soften for 15 minutes. Place 4 roughly chopped ripe tomatoes and 800 g of chopped watermelon in a shallow bowl. Add the onion and vinegar, 1 small handful of mint leaves and 2–3 tablespoons of olive oil. Toss everything together, then crumble over some feta.

8. For a super-simple pesto salad, toss baby spinach and rocket leaves with a handful of basil leaves and toasted pine nuts in a large bowl. In another bowl, mix together a small handful of freshly grated parmesan, the grated zest and juice of a small lemon and 80 ml (⅓ cup) of olive oil. Season to taste with salt and pepper and toss everything together.

PRAWN COCKTAIL SALAD

I always feel nostalgic when I'm told prawn cocktail is on the menu – that classic combination of sweet prawns, tangy sauce, crisp lettuce and creamy avocado is impossible to resist. This retro dish is usually served individually, but I've given my version a generous twist and served it in a large dish for everyone to help themselves. Whether you serve it as an entrée for a special occasion like Christmas or as a main summer salad, prawn cocktail will never go out of fashion.

SERVES: 4   PREP: 20 MINUTES

2 baby cos lettuces, leaves
    separated and torn
1 large handful of watercress sprigs
1 small fennel bulb, finely sliced,
    fronds reserved
1 celery stalk, finely sliced
1 avocado, halved
salt flakes and freshly ground
    black pepper
juice of ¼ lemon
1 kg cooked large prawns, shelled
    and deveined, tails intact

MARIE ROSE SAUCE
3 tablespoons whole-egg
    mayonnaise
2 tablespoons crème fraîche
2 tablespoons tomato sauce
1 teaspoon worcestershire sauce
4 drops of tabasco sauce (or a little
    more for an extra kick)
1 teaspoon brandy
finely grated zest of 1 lemon
salt flakes and freshly ground
    black pepper

For the marie rose sauce, combine the mayonnaise, crème fraîche, tomato sauce, worcestershire and tabasco sauces, brandy and lemon zest in a bowl. Season to taste.

Place the lettuce, watercress, sliced fennel bulb and celery in a large bowl. Scoops chunks of avocado straight from the skin into the bowl. Season with a pinch of salt and pepper and lightly dress with 1 tablespoon of marie rose sauce and the lemon juice. Gently toss with your hands and arrange on a platter.

Arrange the prawns on top of the dressed salad, scatter over the reserved fennel fronds and drizzle over the remaining marie rose sauce. Serve immediately.

PANTRY STAPLES
Brandy
Lemon
Mayonnaise
Salt and pepper
Tabasco sauce
Tomato sauce
Worcestershire
    sauce

SHOPPING LIST
Avocado
Baby cos lettuce
Celery
Crème fraîche
Fennel bulb
Prawns
Watercress

AUNTY VERO'S CRUSTED TOMATOES

I always look forward to my trips to France, particularly my visits to Aunty Vero and Uncle Thierry – both incredible cooks, whose feasts revolve around what they harvest from their amazing veggie patch. Last time I was there, Vero made these crusted tomatoes. Basil and tomato are best mates in any dish and adding the crumb really enforces that perfect combination. These are delicious served as a side to fish, roasted or grilled meat or poached eggs.

SERVES: 4   PREP: 20 MINUTES   COOK: 40 MINUTES

4 truss tomatoes, halved crossways
salt flakes and freshly ground
    black pepper
1 garlic clove, finely chopped
½ small red onion, chopped
4 thyme sprigs, leaves picked
1 handful of basil leaves
2 thick slices of stale sourdough
    bread, crusts removed, torn
2 tablespoons freshly grated
    parmesan
2 tablespoons olive oil

Preheat the oven to 180°C. Line a baking tray with baking paper.

Arrange the tomato halves in a single layer on the prepared tray and season with a pinch of salt and pepper.

Combine the garlic, onion and herbs in a small food processor and pulse four or five times to finely chop. Add the sourdough and parmesan and pulse again until a crumb forms. Add the oil and season with salt and pepper. Pulse again until a paste forms.

Top each tomato half with 1 tablespoon of the breadcrumb mixture, pressing it in with the back of a spoon. Bake for 30–40 minutes until a golden crust forms.

PANTRY STAPLES
Garlic
Olive oil
Parmesan
Red onion
Salt and pepper
Stale sourdough
    bread

SHOPPING LIST
Fresh basil
Fresh thyme
Truss tomatoes

VIETNAMESE TUNA SALAD

This Vietnamese-style salad is a spin-off from the tuna niçoise salad I often have as a speedy mid-week lunch. It evolved from looking in the fridge and pantry to see what I had to create a lunch that wasn't boring. You can do the same and add whatever you have to hand: rice noodles, crispy fried shallots and boiled eggs are all delightful additions. I make up a batch of nuoc cham and keep it in the fridge as it's great to have on standby for salads, rice paper rolls, and as a dipping sauce for barbecued meat.

SERVES: 4   PREP: 15 MINUTES   COOK: 2 MINUTES

2 tablespoons unsalted peanuts, toasted and chopped

2 x 185 g cans tuna in oil, drained and flaked

1 handful each of coriander leaves and mint leaves (or Asian herbs, such as Vietnamese mint and Thai basil)

2 handfuls of mixed salad leaves

½ grapefruit, segmented and chopped

4 cherry tomatoes, quartered

NUOC CHAM

1 small red chilli, finely chopped

1 garlic clove, finely chopped

1 tablespoon fish sauce

1 tablespoon caster sugar

2 tablespoons grapefruit juice

For the nuoc cham, place the chilli, garlic, fish sauce, sugar and 2 tablespoons of water in a small saucepan and bring to the boil. Reduce the heat and simmer for 1–2 minutes, stirring, until the sugar dissolves. Remove from the heat and allow to cool, then add the grapefruit juice.

Crush the peanuts to a crumb with a mortar and pestle.

Place the tuna, herbs, salad leaves, grapefruit segments and tomato in a bowl and pour over the nuoc cham. Toss and scatter over the peanut crumb.

PANTRY STAPLES	SHOPPING LIST
Canned tuna in oil	Cherry tomatoes
Caster sugar	Fresh coriander
Fish sauce	Fresh mint
Garlic	Fresh small red chilli
Unsalted peanuts	Grapefruit
	Mixed salad leaves

SMOKED SALMON AND PICKLED CUCUMBER SALAD

My MasterChef *friend Lucas Parsons cooked a version of this at one of his dinner parties, and it was an absolute hit. His was a little more elaborate than my recipe, but it still has some of the main components. Oily smoked salmon with refreshing cucumber and dill is always a winning combination, but what makes this extra enticing is the fusion of pungent hot English mustard and tangy crème fraîche.*

SERVES: 4   **PREP:** 30 MINUTES, PLUS 1 HOUR 20 MINUTES STANDING AND MARINATING   **COOK:** 5 MINUTES

2 continental cucumbers,
  cut into 5 cm rounds
salt flakes
3 tablespoons white wine vinegar
2 tablespoons sugar
2 teaspoons hot English mustard
4 eggs
2 tablespoons crème fraîche
1 large handful of watercress sprigs
1 small handful of dill sprigs
8 slices of smoked salmon
freshly ground black pepper

Place the cucumber in a colander along with 2 teaspoons of salt and toss. Let stand for 20 minutes. Under a cold running tap, wash the salt off thoroughly, then pat the cucumber dry with a clean tea towel.

Combine the vinegar, sugar and mustard in a bowl and mix until the sugar dissolves. Add the cucumber and toss to coat completely. Place in the fridge for 1 hour to marinate.

Place the eggs in a saucepan and cover with water. Bring to the boil and, once boiling, cook for 3 minutes for soft boiled. Remove the eggs and chill under a running tap, before peeling.

Combine the crème fraîche with 1 teaspoon of the cucumber pickling liquid and a pinch of salt in a bowl.

Place a small handful of watercress and a few sprigs of dill on each serving plate, add some cucumber, then two slices of salmon and a halved egg. Drizzle on the crème fraîche dressing and finish with a grind of black pepper.

PANTRY STAPLES
Eggs
Hot English mustard
Lemon
Salt and pepper
Sugar
White wine vinegar

SHOPPING LIST
Continental
  cucumbers
Crème fraîche
Fresh dill
Smoked salmon
Watercress

SIMPLE CAESAR SALAD

A Caesar would have to be the king of all salads. Its textural perfection and rich creamy sauce make it utterly irresistible. One of my favourite pizza joints in Los Angeles makes their version in a similar way to mine, where the crouton component is served in a crispy crumb form, allowing it to stick to each lettuce leaf. It's also not overly busy – there's no chicken or boiled eggs, making it a lighter salad.

SERVES: 4   PREP: 30 MINUTES   COOK: 15 MINUTES

4 streaky bacon rashers
   (about 120 g), roughly chopped
3 thick slices of stale sourdough
   bread
200 ml grapeseed oil
3 anchovy fillets
1 small garlic clove, peeled
20 g parmesan, finely grated,
   plus extra to serve
1 teaspoon dijon mustard
2 egg yolks
1½ teaspoons red wine vinegar
salt flakes and freshly ground
   black pepper
2 baby cos lettuces,
   leaves separated

Preheat the oven to 180°C. Line a baking tray with baking paper.

Place the bacon in a small food processor and pulse to crumble. Tip out onto the prepared tray. Tear the bread into the food processor bowl and pulse to form breadcrumbs. Tip onto the tray with the bacon and add 2 tablespoons of oil. Use your hands to mix and coat everything in the oil, then spread out evenly over the tray. Bake for 12–15 minutes, checking and tossing a few times to ensure the breadcrumb mixture is crisp and evenly golden. Drain on paper towel.

Combine the anchovies, garlic, 20 g of parmesan, mustard and egg yolks in a jug and blend with a hand-held blender. With the motor running, slowly drizzle in the remaining oil. Once thick and creamy, mix in the vinegar and season with salt and pepper to taste.

In a large bowl or tray, toss the lettuce leaves with half of the dressing and half of the crispy breadcrumb mixture. Top with the remaining breadcrumb mixture and sprinkle over some extra parmesan.

 This makes enough dressing for two salads. Reserve the leftover dressing in an airtight container in the fridge for up to 1 week.

PANTRY STAPLES   **SHOPPING LIST**

Anchovies   Baby cos lettuces
Bacon
Dijon mustard
Eggs
Garlic
Grapeseed oil
Parmesan
Red wine vinegar
Salt and pepper
Stale sourdough
   bread

QUINOA, HALOUMI AND PRUNE SALAD

I love the contrasting tastes of this salad: salty haloumi with sweet and jammy prunes brought together by a sharp vinegary dressing. The juxtaposed flavours make this one of those dishes where you can't wait to have another mouthful.

SERVES: 4   PREP: 20 MINUTES   COOK: 20 MINUTES

100 g (½ cup) tricolour quinoa or
   any quinoa of your choice, rinsed
50 g (⅓ cup) whole almonds,
   toasted and roughly chopped
1 small red onion, very finely sliced
1 large handful each of mint and
   flat-leaf parsley leaves
500 g haloumi, drained and cut
   into 2 cm slices

DRESSING
6 pitted prunes, torn in half
80 ml (⅓ cup) olive oil
1 tablespoon red wine vinegar
salt flakes and freshly ground
   black pepper
juice of 1 orange

To make the dressing, warm the prunes, oil, vinegar and a pinch of salt and pepper in a small saucepan over low heat. The oil should be hot but not smoking. Remove from the heat and set aside to cool and steep for 15 minutes, then stir through the orange juice.

Meanwhile, cook the quinoa as per the packet instructions, then use a fork to separate the grains. Cool to room temperature and place in a bowl along with the nuts, onion and herbs. Reserve 1 teaspoon of the dressing and pour the rest over the quinoa mixture, then toss and mound onto a serving dish.

Heat a large frying pan over medium heat. Drizzle the reserved dressing over the haloumi to lightly coat and fry for 1 minute on each side until golden. Toss the hot haloumi slices through the salad and serve.

PANTRY STAPLES
Almonds
Olive oil
Prunes
Quinoa
Red onion
Red wine vinegar
Salt and pepper

SHOPPING LIST
Fresh flat-leaf
   parsley
Fresh mint
Haloumi
Orange

ROAST BEEF AND BEETROOT SALAD

Beetroot has a sweet, earthy flavour, which marries nicely with beef and a nutty tahini dressing in this deliciously hearty salad. It's an absolute show stopper! This is also great to throw together when you have leftover roast beef or steak, rather than cooking the beef from scratch as I've done here.

SERVES: 4 PREP: 20 MINUTES COOK: 1 HOUR

3 small–medium beetroot
(about 400 g)
1 x 600 g centre-cut beef fillet,
brought to room temperature
2 tablespoons olive oil, plus extra
to serve
salt flakes
½ red onion, finely sliced
2 teaspoons red wine vinegar
freshly ground black pepper
1 large handful of mint leaves
2 tablespoons sesame seeds,
toasted

TAHINI SAUCE
1 garlic clove, finely grated
185 g (¾ cup) Greek yoghurt
2 tablespoons hulled tahini
1 teaspoon ground cumin
2 teaspoons red wine vinegar
salt flakes and freshly ground
black pepper

Preheat the oven to 180°C.

For the tahini sauce, combine the garlic, yoghurt, tahini, cumin and vinegar in a bowl. Season with salt and pepper to taste.

Wash and trim the beetroot, leaving 2 cm of the stem (this makes peeling easier once the beetroot are cooked). Wrap in foil and roast for 50–55 minutes until the beetroot are tender when pierced with a skewer. Set aside until cool enough to handle. While still warm, peel the beetroot (if you have disposable gloves, wear them to protect your hands from staining), then cut each bulb into six wedges.

Meanwhile, rub the beef all over with 1 tablespoon of oil and season generously with salt. Heat an ovenproof frying pan over high heat and sear the meat all over for 4–5 minutes until a crust forms. Place the pan in the oven and roast the beef for 15–20 minutes for rare – roast for a few minutes longer for medium–rare (or longer, depending on how you like your meat cooked). Place the beef on a plate, cover loosely with foil and set aside to rest for 8–10 minutes. Thinly carve the beef.

Place the beetroot in a bowl, add the onion, vinegar and the remaining oil and season with salt and pepper.

To assemble, spread the tahini sauce over a large plate. Arrange the beef on top, then the beetroot and mint. Finish with a sprinkle of sesame seeds and an extra drizzle of olive oil.

PANTRY STAPLES
Garlic
Greek yoghurt
Ground cumin
Olive oil
Red onion
Red wine vinegar
Salt and pepper
Sesame seeds
Tahini

SHOPPING LIST
Beef fillet
Beetroot
Fresh mint

LAMB SHANK AND TOMATO SALAD

*Lamb shank doesn't always have to be served in a rich and hearty sauce. In this recipe,
it's the hero of a delightful tomato, chickpea and feta salad. I often make this at home when
I have leftover shanks or roast lamb from the night before. Simply shred the leftover lamb to
make this into a super-fast salad. Alternatively, serve as part of a wonderful shared platter.*

SERVES: 4   PREP: 20 MINUTES   COOK: 2 HOURS

3 tablespoons olive oil
4 lamb shanks
salt flakes and freshly ground
    black pepper
1 litre chicken stock
1 red onion, finely sliced
½ teaspoon coriander seeds,
    toasted and crushed
1 teaspoon sumac, plus extra
    to serve
1 teaspoon caster sugar
juice of 1 small lemon
1 x 400 g can chickpeas,
    drained and rinsed
4 large tomatoes, cut into
    2 cm chunks
90 g (⅓ cup) Greek yoghurt
1 large handful of flat-leaf
    parsley leaves
1 large handful of mint leaves
150 g feta, crumbled

Preheat the oven to 160°C.

Drizzle a little oil over the shanks and season with salt and pepper.
Heat a flameproof heavy-based casserole dish over medium–high
heat, add the shanks and sear all over until golden. Pour over
the stock and cover with a piece of baking paper cut to fit and
a tight-fitting lid. Transfer to the oven to bake for 2 hours until
the meat falls off the bone easily. Alternatively, you can cook the
lamb in a pressure cooker for 35–40 minutes. Remove the lamb
shanks from the dish and set aside to cool. (Don't throw away the
remaining stock: pour it into a container, cover, cool and freeze.
It will keep for up to 3 months in the freezer.) When the lamb
is cool enough to handle, shred into chunks, discarding any fat,
sinew and bone.

Place the onion, coriander seeds, sumac, sugar, lemon juice and
a good pinch of salt in a large bowl. Mix together, then set aside
to allow the onion to pickle for 10–15 minutes.

Add the remaining oil to the pickled onion and mix to incorporate.
Taste: it should be zingy! Add the lamb, chickpeas and tomato and
toss to coat.

To assemble, spread the yoghurt over the base of a large shallow
dish. Immediately before serving, add the herbs to the lamb salad
and toss one final time. Check the seasoning, then arrange the
salad on top of the yoghurt and crumble over the feta. Season
with some extra sumac and serve.

✻ Serve with some Lebanese bread, if you like.

PANTRY STAPLES
Canned chickpeas
Caster sugar
Chicken stock
Coriander seeds
Feta
Greek yoghurt
Lemon
Olive oil
Red onion
Salt and pepper
Sumac

SHOPPING LIST
Fresh flat-leaf
    parsley
Fresh mint
Lamb shanks
Tomatoes

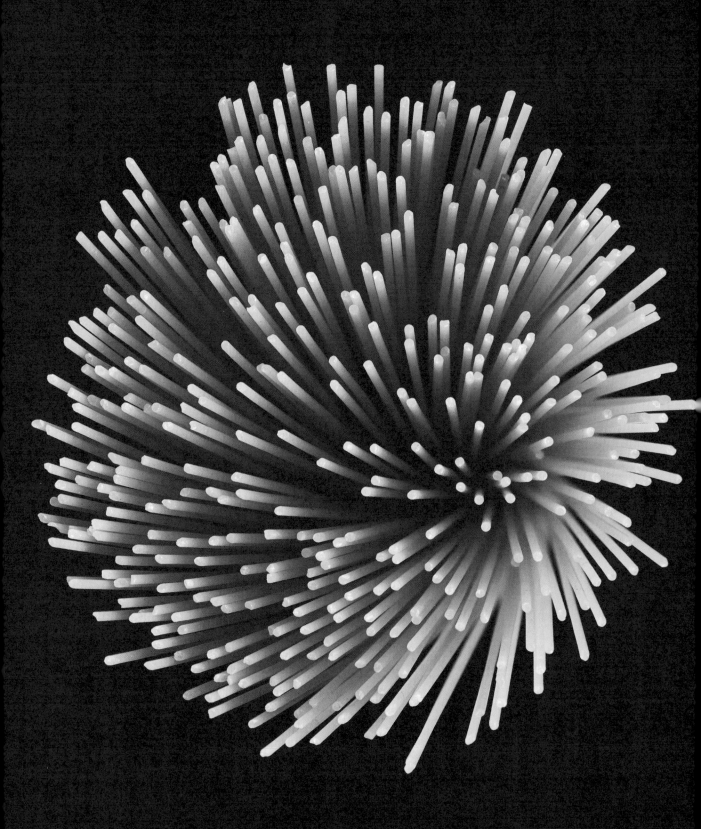

PASTA & NOODLES

FUSILLI WITH CAPSICUM AND SUN-DRIED TOMATO PESTO

We all know and love the celebrated basil pesto from Genoa, but there are many different ways to make it – like this one created with semi-dried tomatoes and thickened with almonds. I also include jarred roasted capsicum to impart a lovely sweetness and rich red colour. This is the perfect weeknight pasta dish, designed around ingredients with a long shelf life. I use semi-dried tomatoes because I prefer their sweet taste; if you want a deeper flavour, use sun-dried tomatoes.

SERVES: 4   PREP: 15 MINUTES   COOK: 15 MINUTES

500 g fusilli (or any pasta shape of your choice)
80 ml (⅓ cup) olive oil
1 garlic clove, sliced
4 flat-leaf parsley sprigs, leaves picked and roughly chopped, stalks reserved
200 g semi-dried tomatoes
100 g jarred roasted red capsicum, drained and roughly chopped
50 g (⅓ cup) blanched almonds
3 tablespoons grated pecorino or parmesan
1 fresh mozzarella ball, torn
salt flakes and freshly ground black pepper

Bring a large saucepan of salted water to the boil, add the pasta and cook until al dente. Drain, reserving 80 ml (⅓ cup) of cooking water.

Meanwhile, heat the oil in a frying pan over medium heat, add the garlic and parsley stalks and cook for 1 minute until the garlic just begins to change colour. Add the tomatoes and capsicum, stir to coat in the oil and cook for 1–2 minutes to warm through. Place in a food processor or blender, add the almonds, cheese and reserved pasta cooking water and blend until a smooth paste forms.

Place the pesto in the pasta pan. Return the drained pasta to the pan and add half the mozzarella and most of the parsley leaves. Toss so the pasta is completely coated and season with salt and pepper. Serve with the remaining mozzarella on top and a last sprinkle of parsley leaves.

PANTRY STAPLES

Blanched almonds
Fusilli pasta
Garlic
Jarred roasted red capsicum
Olive oil
Pecorino or parmesan
Salt and pepper

SHOPPING LIST

Fresh flat-leaf parsley
Mozzarella ball
Semi-dried tomatoes

SPINACH GNUDI

Incredibly light and fluffy, these gnudi are like little bundles of cloud. The trick is not to use too much flour, but rather create a translucent casing by rolling the spinach and ricotta mixture in it. To ensure they don't break up, it's really important to let the gnudi chill before cooking.

SERVES: 6   PREP: 30 MINUTES, PLUS AT LEAST 1 HOUR CHILLING
COOK: 15 MINUTES   SUITABLE TO FREEZE

500 g frozen spinach, thawed
500 g (2 cups) fresh, full-fat
ricotta, drained
1 egg
30 g (heaped ¼ cup) finely grated
parmesan, plus extra to serve
pinch of freshly grated nutmeg,
plus extra to serve
150 g (1 cup) plain flour (ideally
Tipo 00), plus extra for dusting
salt flakes and freshly ground
black pepper
80 g butter
1 large handful of sage leaves

Place the spinach in a colander and squeeze out as much liquid as possible. Transfer to a food processor and pulse three or four times to finely chop. Add the ricotta, egg, parmesan, nutmeg, 1 tablespoon of flour and a pinch of salt and pepper and pulse two or three times until the mixture just comes together and forms a sticky dough.

Line a tray with baking paper and dust with a little flour. Tip the remaining flour into a shallow dish and, with lightly floured hands and using a tablespoon as a rough guide, shape portions of the dough into round gnudi (dumplings). Gently toss in the flour to completely coat, then roll into balls and arrange on the prepared tray in a single layer. Place in the fridge to firm up for 1 hour or, even better, overnight.

Place the butter in a small saucepan over medium–low heat until it starts to foam. Continue to cook until the butter browns slightly and smells nutty (noisette stage), then add the sage and remove from the heat.

Bring a large saucepan of salted water to a gentle boil. (If the water is rapidly boiling, the delicate gnudi will break up.) Add the gnudi in two batches and poach for 2–3 minutes until they rise to the surface. Remove the gnudi with a slotted spoon and arrange five or six on each serving plate. Drizzle over the butter, add a few sage leaves and serve with a sprinkle of extra nutmeg and parmesan.

✳ The gnudi can be made a day or two ahead. Simply cover the gnudi on the tray with plastic wrap and place in the fridge until you are ready to cook them. Or they can be frozen in an airtight container for up to a month. If freezing, place a piece of baking paper between each layer of gnudi. When ready to eat, plunge the gnudi straight from the freezer into a saucepan of simmering salted water.

These gnudi are also great with a roasted tomato sauce (page 66).

I've also tested these with fine polenta instead of flour and it works really well. So all my gluten-intolerant friends out there can enjoy these, too.

PANTRY STAPLES   **SHOPPING LIST**

Butter   Fresh sage
Egg
Frozen spinach
Nutmeg
Parmesan
Plain flour
Ricotta
Salt and pepper

PENNE WITH ZUCCHINI CREMA

This is a much-loved pasta dish in my repertoire. It's amazing how adaptable zucchini are and I love the way they can be transformed depending on how you cook them. Here, the zucchini are cooked until very soft and creamy, making this super light yet very moreish. It's easy to whip for a weeknight dinner, particularly if you're looking for a champion vegetarian meal that everyone will love.

SERVES: 4   PREP: 10 MINUTES   COOK: 25 MINUTES   SUITABLE TO FREEZE

500 g penne (or any tubular pasta of your choice)
80 ml (⅓ cup) olive oil
1 garlic clove, peeled and bruised
2–3 small zucchini (about 400 g), cut into 5 mm thick rounds
1 small handful of basil leaves
1 small handful of mint leaves
1½ tablespoons pine nuts
20 g parmesan, finely grated, plus extra to serve
salt flakes and freshly ground black pepper

Bring a large saucepan of salted water to the boil, add the pasta and cook until just al dente.

While the pasta is cooking, heat 2 tablespoons of oil in a large sauté pan over medium–high heat. Add the garlic and zucchini, toss to coat the zucchini in the oil and cook for 3–4 minutes to soften and colour a little. Add 500 ml (2 cups) of water and cook for 12–15 minutes until the zucchini is tender and the water has evaporated.

Transfer the zucchini and garlic to a blender, add the herbs, pine nuts, parmesan and salt and pepper and blend until smooth and silky. Add the remaining oil and blend again.

Drain the pasta and place back in the pan. Add the zucchini crema and toss to coat completely. Serve with the extra parmesan and a sprinkle of pepper.

 The zucchini crema freezes well in an airtight container. Simply thaw and reheat, then fold through freshly cooked pasta.

PANTRY STAPLES
Garlic
Olive oil
Parmesan
Penne
Pine nuts
Salt and pepper

SHOPPING LIST
Fresh basil
Fresh mint
Zucchini

WHOLEMEAL SPAGHETTI WITH KALE AND RICOTTA

Kale can sometimes be a bit ordinary eaten on its own; however, when spiked with chilli and vinegar and a pop of sweetness from raisins, it's brought to life. Serve with wholemeal pasta to give a wonderful nutty flavour, top with ricotta for creaminess and you have a brilliant home-cooked pasta dish in minutes.

SERVES: 2   PREP: 10 MINUTES   COOK: 15 MINUTES

1 bunch of kale (about 500 g), stalks removed, leaves chopped into 2.5 cm pieces
250 g wholemeal spaghetti
3 tablespoons olive oil, plus extra for drizzling
1 red onion, finely sliced
1 tablespoon raisins
½ teaspoon chilli flakes
salt flakes and freshly ground black pepper
1 tablespoon balsamic vinegar
3 tablespoons fresh, full-fat ricotta

Bring a large saucepan of salted water to the boil. Add the kale and cook until the water comes back to the boil. Boil for 3 minutes, then remove the kale with a slotted spoon and transfer to a plate. Bring the water back up to the boil, add the spaghetti and cook until just al dente. Drain, reserving some of the cooking water.

While the pasta is cooking, heat the oil in a large frying pan over medium heat. Add the onion and fry for 3–4 minutes until caramelised. Stir in the raisins and chilli flakes, then add the kale and toss through. Season with salt and pepper, then add the balsamic, pasta and a few tablespoons of the reserved pasta water. Toss and portion the pasta into shallow bowls. Dollop the ricotta over the top, drizzle on a little extra oil and finish with a sprinkle of pepper.

PANTRY STAPLES
Balsamic vinegar
Chilli flakes
Olive oil
Raisins
Red onion
Ricotta
Salt and pepper
Wholemeal spaghetti

SHOPPING LIST
Kale

EGGPLANT PUTTANESCA

*I couldn't decide which dish to include in this book: pasta alla Norma (an eggplant-
and tomato-based sauce) or puttanesca (a fiery sauce consisting of tomatoes, black olives
and chilli). Because of my indecisiveness, I ended up with a real hybrid; the two have become
one and the result is fantastic. I make this once a week, I love it that much!*

SERVES: 4   **PREP:** 10 MINUTES   **COOK:** 20 MINUTES

100 ml olive oil
1 eggplant, peeled and cut into
   1 cm dice
salt flakes
4 anchovy fillets, finely chopped
2 garlic cloves, finely chopped
¼ teaspoon chilli flakes, or to taste
1 x 400 g can whole peeled
   tomatoes, crushed
60 g pitted black olives, halved
1 tablespoon baby capers in brine,
   drained
500 g rigatoni (or any pasta shape
   of your choice)
1 small handful of finely grated
   parmesan or pecorino, plus extra
   to serve
freshly ground black pepper

Heat 80 ml (⅓ cup) of oil in a large frying pan over medium–high heat. Add the eggplant and toss in the oil, then season with a small pinch of salt and fry for 3–4 minutes until softened and lightly coloured. Add the remaining oil, the anchovy, garlic and chilli and cook for a further 30 seconds until fragrant. Tip in the tomatoes and stir to coat the eggplant, then add the olives and capers. Simmer for 3–4 minutes until the sauce is thick and rich.

Meanwhile, bring a large saucepan of salted water to the boil. Add the pasta and cook until al dente. Using tongs, shake the excess water off the pasta and drop directly into the sauce. Sprinkle over the cheese and toss to completely coat the pasta in the sauce. Serve with a grind of pepper and a sprinkle of extra cheese.

PANTRY STAPLES
Anchovies
Canned whole
   peeled tomatoes
Capers
Chilli flakes
Garlic
Olive oil
Parmesan or
   pecorino
Rigatoni
Salt and pepper

SHOPPING LIST
Eggplant
Pitted black olives

ZUCCHINI AND PRAWN PASTA

For a dish that takes only 15 minutes to cook, this is seriously good. I love to whip this up when I have friends over in the middle of the week, don't have hours to spend in the kitchen and still want to make them something impressive. I chop my prawns, as opposed to leaving them whole, so with every mouthful of pasta you can taste their sweetness.

SERVES: 4   PREP: 15 MINUTES   COOK: 15 MINUTES

2 small zucchini (about 250 g)
400 g spaghetti
3 tablespoons olive oil
2 garlic cloves, chopped
1 small red chilli, finely chopped
250 g cherry tomatoes, halved
600 g raw medium prawns, shelled,
    deveined and chopped
salt flakes and freshly ground
    black pepper
150 ml white wine
finely grated zest of 1 lemon
1 small handful of flat-leaf
    parsley leaves

Using a vegetable peeler, peel the zucchini into long thin ribbons. Group them into bundles of four and finely slice lengthways so they resemble spaghetti. Alternatively, coarsely grate on a box grater or use a spiraliser.

Bring a large saucepan of salted water to the boil, add the pasta and cook until just al dente.

While the pasta is cooking, heat the oil in a large sauté pan over medium–high heat. Add the garlic and chilli, toss to coat in the oil and cook for about 30 seconds until fragrant. Add the tomato and zucchini, toss again and cook for 1–2 minutes. Add the prawn meat, season with salt and pepper and cook for 30 seconds. Pour in the wine and bring to the boil, then cook for a further 3–4 minutes.

Drain the pasta and add to the zucchini mixture along with the lemon zest and parsley. Toss again to completely coat the pasta in the sauce and serve immediately.

PANTRY STAPLES
Garlic
Lemon
Olive oil
Salt and pepper
Spaghetti
White wine

SHOPPING LIST
Cherry tomatoes
Fresh flat-leaf
    parsley
Fresh small red chilli
Prawns
Zucchini

CASARECCE WITH GORGONZOLA, SPECK AND WALNUTS

This decadent pasta is a true example of how three main ingredients can work so well together. I use a mild gorgonzola that is sweet and creamy so it doesn't overwhelm the spiced and lightly smoked speck. The toasted walnuts impart a crunch and a wonderful nutty flavour that makes this a unique and mouth-watering dish. If you can't find speck, you can use pancetta or good-quality streaky bacon.

SERVES: 4   **PREP:** 5 MINUTES   **COOK:** 15 MINUTES

500 g casarecce (or any short
  pasta of your choice)
150 g speck, rind removed,
  cut into lardons
250 g Gorgonzola Dolce cheese
2 tablespoons milk
salt flakes and freshly ground
  black pepper
30 g parmesan, finely grated
50 g (½ cup) walnuts, toasted
  and chopped

Bring a large saucepan of salted water to the boil, add the pasta and cook until just al dente.

While the pasta is cooking, add the speck to a large frying pan and place over medium heat. Cook, stirring occasionally, for 5–6 minutes until the fat renders and the speck is crisp. Drain on paper towel. Wipe the pan clean.

Combine the gorgonzola and milk in the clean pan and place over medium–low heat. Cook, stirring regularly to ensure the mixture doesn't split, until the gorgonzola melts. Add two-thirds of the speck and season with pepper and a small pinch of salt (the cheese and speck should be salty enough).

Drain the pasta, add to the sauce with the parmesan and toss to coat. Portion the pasta into serving bowls and top with the remaining speck and walnuts. Finish with a final grind of pepper.

PANTRY STAPLES

Casarecce
Milk
Parmesan
Salt and pepper
Walnuts

SHOPPING LIST

Gorgonzola Dolce
  cheese
Speck

SPAGHETTI VONGOLE

Spaghetti vongole, in all its glory, is ridiculously easy. It's a dish that requires minimal ingredients and perfect timing. I suggest having everything sliced and ready to go before you begin, so you can have a seamless cook. For a textural twist, I add crispy fried breadcrumbs (or poor man's parmesan, as it's called in Italy) but you can leave out this component if you want to make this dish from start to finish in the time it takes to cook the pasta.

SERVES: 4   PREP: 15 MINUTES   COOK: 15 MINUTES

2 thick slices of stale sourdough bread, crusts removed
125 ml (½ cup) olive oil
400 g spaghetti or linguine
1 kg vongole (clams), soaked in water for 20 minutes (unless bought ready purged and pot ready)
2 garlic cloves, finely sliced
1 long red chilli, finely sliced
100 ml white wine (such as chardonnay or sauvignon blanc)
1 large handful of flat-leaf parsley leaves, roughly chopped
salt flakes and freshly ground black pepper

Place the sourdough in a food processor and pulse until fine crumbs form.

Heat 3 tablespoons of oil in a large sauté pan over medium heat and add the breadcrumbs. Toss to coat the crumbs in the oil and cook, tossing constantly, for 3–4 minutes until the crumbs are crisp and golden. Drain on paper towel and set aside. Wipe the pan clean.

Bring a large saucepan of salted water to the boil, add the pasta and cook until just al dente.

While the pasta is cooking, heat the remaining oil in the clean pan over high heat, add the vongole, garlic and chilli and toss. Pour in the wine, cover with a lid and cook for 1–2 minutes until the vongole start to open.

Drain the pasta, reserving a few tablespoons of the cooking water, and add to the vongole along with the parsley. Toss to coat the pasta in the lovely juices, adding the reserved pasta water if required. Taste and check the seasoning, adding a little salt and pepper if required. Pour into a large shallow dish and scatter over the crispy breadcrumbs.

PANTRY STAPLES
Garlic
Olive oil
Salt and pepper
Spaghetti or linguine
Stale sourdough bread
White wine

SHOPPING LIST
Fresh flat-leaf parsley
Fresh long red chilli
Vongole (clams)

EASY PASTA COMBOS

1. Soak a small handful of dried porcini mushrooms in 185 ml of hot water. Heat some olive oil in a large frying pan over high heat. Add 250 g of mushrooms and 3 chopped rashers of bacon. Cook for 3–4 minutes until golden. Squeeze the water out of the porcini and reserve the liquid. Add the porcini to the pan. Season. Pour in the reserved liquid. Reduce by one-third before adding 150 ml of cream. Simmer for 30 seconds until the sauce is thick enough to coat the back of a spoon. Toss through al dente pasta.

2. For a super-speedy carbonara, heat 1 tablespoon of olive oil in a large frying pan over low heat. Add 300 g of chopped pancetta. Cook for 5–8 minutes until crispy. Whisk 1 egg, 4 egg yolks, 80 g of finely grated parmesan and a pinch of salt and pepper in a bowl. Add 500 g of al dente spaghetti and 125 ml (½ cup) of pasta cooking water to the pan. Toss to coat. Remove from the heat. Tip on the egg and cheese mixture. Toss thoroughly to coat the pasta with the cream-like sauce. Serve with extra pepper.

3. For quick noodle bowls, marinate 4 lean pork chops in soy sauce, Chinese five spice and sesame oil. Chargrill for a few minutes on each side. Slice and serve with rice vermicelli, fresh Asian herbs and grated carrot and cucumber, and drizzle over some nuoc cham (page 33).

4. Fry a finely chopped onion in olive oil in a large frying pan until softened. Deglaze with 3 tablespoons of white wine and reduce by one-third. Stir in 200 g of crème fraîche or sour cream. Simmer until thick. Add al dente pasta and a few tablespoons of pasta cooking water to the pan, then toss. Scatter over the grated zest of 1 lemon and 185 g of flaked hot-smoked salmon. Toss again and serve.

5. For a vegetarian 'bolognese', heat 80 ml (⅓ cup) of olive oil in a large frying pan. Add 800 g of finely chopped mixed mushrooms, some finely chopped onion and garlic and a pinch of chilli flakes. Fry for 10–15 minutes. Deglaze with 125 ml (½ cup) of red wine. Tip in a 400 g can of chopped tomatoes and a little water. Season with salt. Cook for 20 minutes until rich and thick. Toss through al dente pasta and serve with grated parmesan.

6. Squeeze 600 g of good-quality sausage meat from their casings into a sauté pan. Fry in a few tablespoons of olive oil, breaking up into small chunks with a wooden spoon. Add a finely chopped garlic clove, ½ teaspoon of fennel seeds and a roughly chopped bunch of broccolini. Pour in 3 tablespoons of white wine and reduce by one-third. Add 125 ml (½ cup) of chicken stock and cook for a few minutes. Add al dente pasta, a large handful of parmesan and toss.

7. Heat a tablespoon of olive oil in an ovenproof frying pan over medium heat. Add a finely chopped onion and garlic clove. Fry until softened. Pour in 700 g of tomato passata. Add a pinch of salt and pepper. Bring to the boil. Cook for 15 minutes to thicken. Add 1 cup of shredded barbecued chicken, a large handful of basil leaves, al dente pasta of your choice and a little pasta cooking water. Toss. Fold through a large handful of grated parmesan and a torn large mozzarella ball. Top with breadcrumbs, drizzle with olive oil and bake at 200°C for 15–20 minutes.

LEFTOVER CHICKEN AND SOBA NOODLE SALAD

Roast chook never goes to waste in my house as there are countless ways to produce new dishes from leftovers, like this yummy salad with soba noodles and a fragrant ginger dressing. I use snow peas and spring onions in my recipe but it's all about adapting, so change it up depending on what you love and have on hand.

SERVES: 2   PREP: 20 MINUTES   COOK: 5 MINUTES

270 g soba noodles

½ roast chicken, fat and bones discarded, meat shredded

4 spring onions, finely sliced

1 large handful of snow peas (about 150 g), topped and tailed, finely sliced

150 g edamame beans, blanched and podded

2 tablespoons sesame seeds, toasted, plus 1 teaspoon extra to serve

DRESSING

3 cm piece of ginger, finely chopped

3 tablespoons soy sauce

3 tablespoons rice wine vinegar

1 tablespoon caster sugar

1 tablespoon sesame oil

To make the dressing, place all the ingredients in a jar, add 1 tablespoon of water, cover and shake to combine.

Bring a large saucepan of water to the boil and cook the soba noodles as per the packet instructions. Drain and refresh under cold water.

In a large bowl, combine the chicken, noodles, spring onion, snow peas, edamame and sesame seeds. Pour three-quarters of the dressing over the salad and toss. Add the remaining dressing and toss again. Scatter over the extra sesame seeds and serve.

 Edamame can be found in the freezer section of Asian grocers and selected supermarkets. Peas are a great substitute here.

PANTRY STAPLES

Caster sugar
Fresh ginger
Rice wine vinegar
Sesame oil
Sesame seeds
Soba noodles
Soy sauce

SHOPPING LIST

Edamame beans
Roast chicken
Snow peas
Spring onions

BASIC ROASTED TOMATO AND BASIL SAUCE

When tomatoes are at their peak, I love to make big batches of this sauce and freeze it. The best tomatoes to use are over-ripe ones, so keep your eyes peeled at the greengrocer in the section where they've slashed prices to get rid of damaged or imperfect fruit and vegetables. Enjoy this sauce tossed through freshly cooked, al dente spaghetti with a generous sprinkling of parmesan. Ah, the simple things are always so rewarding.

SERVES: 4   PREP: 15 MINUTES   COOK: 55 MINUTES   SUITABLE TO FREEZE

1 kg roma tomatoes
salt flakes
3 tablespoons olive oil
2 garlic cloves, chopped
1 tablespoon tomato paste
1 large handful of basil leaves
freshly grated parmesan or
    pecorino, to serve
freshly ground black pepper

PANTRY STAPLES   **SHOPPING LIST**
Garlic   Fresh basil
Olive oil   Roma tomatoes
Parmesan or
    pecorino
Salt and pepper
Tomato paste

Preheat the oven to 180°C.

Cut the tomatoes in half lengthways and squeeze out some of the seeds. Place the tomatoes, cut-side up, on a baking tray, season with salt and drizzle over 1 tablespoon of oil. Roast for 40–45 minutes, turning halfway through, until the tomato halves are softened and their skins are shrivelled. Set aside to cool a little, then, using tongs, remove and discard the skins.

Heat the remaining oil in a large sauté pan over medium heat, add the garlic and cook for a few seconds before adding the tomato paste. Cook for a further minute, then add the roasted tomatoes and any juices that have gathered on the tray. Bring to the boil, using a wooden spoon to break up the tomatoes. Cook for a further 4–5 minutes, then add the basil and stir through to wilt a little. Serve with a generous sprinkle of cheese and pepper.

* For a speedier sauce, replace the fresh tomatoes with 2 x 400 g cans of whole peeled tomatoes. Add them to the pan after the tomato paste and cook for 10–15 minutes.

TAGLIATELLE WITH CRÈME FRAÎCHE AND PROSCIUTTO

Now that crème fraîche is readily available in our supermarkets, I've started creating more and more recipes with it. Its rich and tangy flavour makes it the ideal ingredient to add to a fast pasta dish. Combined with sweet baby peas, fragrant mint and salty prosciutto it's the perfect spring meal. I use fresh tagliatelle for my recipe, but it's just as delicious with dried fettuccine.

SERVES: 2   **PREP:** 5 MINUTES   **COOK:** 15 MINUTES

1 tablespoon olive oil
½ onion, finely chopped
100 g (¾ cup) frozen baby peas
125 ml (½ cup) dry white wine (such as chardonnay or sauvignon blanc)
200 g crème fraîche
salt flakes and freshly ground black pepper
250 g fresh or dried tagliatelle
1 handful of finely grated parmesan
1 small handful of mint leaves
6 very thin slices of prosciutto

Heat the oil in a sauté pan over medium heat, add the onion and cook, stirring regularly, for 3–4 minutes until softened but not coloured. Turn up the heat to medium–high and add the peas. Toss, coating the peas in the oil and onion, and cook for 1 minute before adding the wine. Simmer until the liquid is reduced by one-third. Add the crème fraîche and simmer for 2–3 minutes until the sauce thickens slightly. Taste and season with salt and pepper.

Meanwhile, bring a large saucepan of salted water to the boil, add the pasta and cook until just al dente. Drain and add to the cream sauce, along with the cheese, mint and a few tablespoons of the pasta cooking water. Toss until each strand of pasta is coated in the sauce. Portion the pasta into shallow bowls and cover with the prosciutto.

PANTRY STAPLES
Frozen baby peas
Olive oil
Onion
Parmesan
Salt and pepper
White wine

SHOPPING LIST
Crème fraîche
Fresh mint
Fresh or dried tagliatelle
Prosciutto

PENNE WITH TOMATO RELISH AND CHORIZO

Relish in pasta? Bizarre, I know, but this dish was one of my friend Pedro's bestsellers when he was head chef at a restaurant we both worked at 12 years ago. The reason it works so well is the contrast in flavours: sweet, spicy and vinegary relish plays off nicely with the salty chorizo and parmesan. I love the idea of having a few exciting ingredients – such as curry leaves, chorizo and relish – on standby in the freezer, fridge or pantry so a delicious dish like this can be made quickly.

SERVES: 2   PREP: 10 MINUTES   COOK: 15 MINUTES

250 g penne (or any pasta shape of your choice)
1 tablespoon olive oil
1 chorizo sausage, sliced
1 garlic clove, finely chopped
6 fresh or 4 dried curry leaves
1 tablespoon tomato relish
1 large tomato, chopped
salt flakes and freshly ground black pepper
100 ml white wine (such as chardonnay or sauvignon blanc)
1 small handful of flat-leaf parsley leaves, finely chopped (optional)
30 g parmesan, freshly shaved

Bring a large saucepan of salted water to the boil, add the pasta and cook until just al dente.

While the pasta is cooking, heat the oil in a large frying pan over medium heat and add the chorizo. Cook for 2–3 minutes until the oil from the chorizo is released. Add the garlic and curry leaves and stir to coat in the oil, then add the relish and tomato. Season with salt and pepper, stir and cook for a further 30 seconds to soften the tomato. Deglaze with the wine, then bring to a simmer and cook for 2–3 minutes.

Drain the pasta and add to the sauce with 1–2 tablespoons of the pasta cooking water. Add the parsley, if using, and toss everything together. Finish with a good grind of black pepper and serve with the parmesan.

PANTRY STAPLES

Chorizo sausage
Curry leaves
Garlic
Olive oil
Parmesan
Penne
Salt and pepper
Tomato relish
White wine

SHOPPING LIST

Fresh flat-leaf parsley
Tomato

SHORT-CUT SPAGHETTI AND MEATBALLS

Making authentic nonna-style meatballs usually involves a long list of ingredients. Here, I've cut that list right back so you can have a comforting bowl of spaghetti and meatballs any day of the week. The trick is to use good-quality Italian-style pork sausages flavoured with fennel, chilli, garlic and herbs and nicely balanced with fat (so they'll stay moist when cooked). My local butcher makes great sausages and I always get extra and freeze some, making whipping up this dish is as easy as clicking my fingers.

SERVES: 4   PREP: 15 MINUTES   COOK: 35 MINUTES

750 g thick pork and fennel
   sausages
2 tablespoons olive oil
1 onion, finely chopped
700 g tomato passata
1 handful of basil leaves
salt flakes and freshly ground
   black pepper
500 g spaghetti
2 handfuls of freshly grated
   parmesan

Squeeze the sausage meat from the casings in 3 cm lengths and roll into mini meatballs (about 2.5 cm).

Heat the oil in a large sauté pan over medium–high heat and add the meatballs in a single layer. Fry for 3–4 minutes until golden brown all over. Remove from the pan.

Add the onion to the pan and fry, stirring occasionally, for 2–3 minutes to soften. Pour in the passata and bring to the boil. Turn down the heat to low, then return the meatballs to the pan and add the basil and a pinch of salt and pepper. Spoon the sauce over to completely submerge the meatballs, then cover with a lid and cook, stirring occasionally, for 20–25 minutes. Remove the lid and simmer for a further 5 minutes to thicken the sauce.

Meanwhile, bring a large saucepan of salted water to the boil, add the spaghetti and cook until just al dente. Drain and return to the pan. Add two-thirds of the meatballs and sauce and toss through to coat the spaghetti. Transfer to a serving platter and pour over the remaining sauce and meatballs. Serve sprinkled with the parmesan.

 For a touch of heat, add a halved small red chilli.

PANTRY STAPLES   **SHOPPING LIST**

Olive oil   Fresh basil
Onion
Parmesan
Salt and pepper
Sausages
Spaghetti
Tomato passata

PANCETTA, CHICKPEA AND CHILLI SHELLS

Having a can of chickpeas on standby is great for a quick pasta dinner like this one.
The chickpeas offer a creamy and nutty quality to the dish and the pancetta imparts
a wonderful saltiness. Perfect for four or double the recipe for a crowd.

SERVES: 4   **PREP:** 10 MINUTES   **COOK:** 15 MINUTES

400 g shell-shaped pasta (or any
   pasta shape of your choice)
2 tablespoons olive oil
1 x 200 g piece of flat pancetta,
   cut into lardons
1 small rosemary sprig
1 garlic clove, finely chopped
2 long red chillies, finely chopped
1 x 400 g can chickpeas, rinsed
   and drained
2 tablespoons tomato paste
125 ml (½ cup) white wine (such as
   chardonnay or sauvignon blanc)
salt flakes
30 g parmesan, freshly grated

Bring a large saucepan of salted water to the boil. Add the pasta and cook until just al dente.

While the pasta is cooking, heat the oil in a large frying pan over medium–high heat and add the pancetta. Cook for 2–3 minutes until golden. Add the rosemary, garlic and chilli and cook for a further minute before adding the chickpeas and tomato paste. Stir to coat the chickpeas in the tomato paste, then deglaze the pan with the wine. Bring to the boil and simmer for 1 minute.

Drain the pasta and add to the sauce, along with 125 ml (½ cup) of the pasta cooking water. Toss to completely coat the pasta in the sauce. Remove the rosemary sprig, taste and season with salt. Serve with the grated parmesan.

✱ You can use speck or streaky bacon instead of the pancetta, if you like.

PANTRY STAPLES
Canned chickpeas
Garlic
Olive oil
Parmesan
Salt
Shell-shaped pasta
Tomato paste
White wine

SHOPPING LIST
Fresh long red
   chillies
Fresh rosemary
Pancetta

PORK AND PEANUT BUTTER HOKKIEN NOODLES

This is a rich and delicious noodle dish that deviates from a traditional stir-fry with the addition of peanut butter. Crunchy peanut butter is a wonderful ingredient to have in the pantry as, when used in a savoury recipe like this, it adds a sweet, salty and nutty flavour along with a thick, creamy texture that brings the whole dish together.

SERVES: 4   PREP: 15 MINUTES   COOK: 15 MINUTES

250 g thin hokkien noodles
1 tablespoon peanut oil
1 x 400 g pork fillet, trimmed
    and sliced as thinly as possible
    (about 3 mm thick)
salt flakes
1 small handful of garlic chives,
    snipped into 2 cm lengths
2 handfuls of bean sprouts
1 handful of toasted unsalted
    peanuts
lemon wedges, to serve

SAUCE
125 g (½ cup) crunchy
    peanut butter
2 tablespoons soy sauce
1 teaspoon honey
juice of ½ lemon
pinch of chilli powder or
    chilli flakes
1 garlic clove, finely grated

To make the sauce, combine all the ingredients in a small saucepan, add 125 ml (½ cup) of water and whisk over medium heat until smooth and the consistency of thickened cream. If the sauce is too thick, add a little extra water.

Prepare the noodles as per the packet instructions. Drain and place in a large bowl.

Drizzle the oil over the pork, season with salt and massage in with your hands.

Heat a large non-stick frying pan over high heat and stir-fry the pork in batches (so the pan is not overcrowded) for 30–60 seconds on each side until nicely charred.

Add the pork, most of the chives, the sauce and 1 handful of bean sprouts to the noodles. Toss until the noodles and pork are coated in the sauce. Arrange the noodle mixture on a serving platter, scatter over the peanuts and remaining bean sprouts and serve with the remaining chives sprinkled over the top and the lemon wedges on the side.

PANTRY STAPLES
Chilli powder or
    chilli flakes
Garlic
Hokkien noodles
Honey
Lemons
Peanut butter
Peanut oil
Peanuts
Salt
Soy sauce

SHOPPING LIST
Bean sprouts
Garlic chives
Pork fillet

BAKE

STUFFED SUMMER VEGETABLES

On a recent trip to Greece I fell in love with a stuffed vegetable dish called 'yemista'. Usually filled with rice, my version uses couscous and cheese and whatever leftovers I have on hand. I also add a green sauce for drizzling, as I love its vibrant flavour. Other vegetables suitable for stuffing include zucchini, tomato, eggplant and potato. Mashed veggies, rissoles (Silverbeet Polpettine on page 83) or risotto (page 121) work nicely for the filling, too. This is truly a feast for the eyes.

SERVES: 4   PREP: 30 MINUTES   COOK: 1 HOUR 15 MINUTES

2 large onions, peeled
4 small capsicums (green, red
    or yellow)
170 ml (⅔ cup) extra-virgin olive oil
200 g (1 cup) instant couscous
1 x 400 g can lentils, drained
    and rinsed
75 g soft goat's cheese, crumbled
200 g (1 cup) fresh, full-fat ricotta
50 g (½ cup) walnuts, chopped,
    plus extra 20 g, finely chopped
½ teaspoon ground allspice
finely grated zest and juice
    of 1 lemon
salt flakes and freshly ground
    black pepper
1 tablespoon baby capers in brine,
    drained and chopped
1 large handful of flat-leaf parsley
    leaves, finely chopped
1 handful of basil leaves,
    finely chopped

Bring a saucepan of water to the boil. Cut a thin 1 cm deep wedge from each onion (this helps the onion layers separate as they cook). Add the onions to the boiling water and cook for 10–15 minutes until softened. Remove with a slotted spoon and allow to cool. When cool enough to handle, carefully peel away each softened outer layer and set aside. Finely chop the remaining inner part of the onion and reserve.

Remove the tops of the capsicums, then, with a spoon, carefully scoop out and discard the seeds and membrane, ensuring you do not pierce the skin. Keep the tops.

Preheat the oven to 180°C. Grease a shallow baking dish with 1 teaspoon of the oil.

Cook the couscous as per the packet instructions. Add the lentils, cheeses, chopped walnuts, allspice, lemon zest and the reserved chopped onion. Season well.

Fill the cavity of each capsicum with the couscous mixture and place the reserved lids on top. Place in the prepared baking dish. Spoon a dessertspoon of the couscous mixture into the centre of each onion layer, then roll up to form a seashell shape. Place, seam-side down, in the baking dish with the capsicum. Drizzle over 80 ml (⅓ cup) of oil and season well with salt and pepper. Bake for 1 hour until the vegetables are lightly caramelised.

In the meantime, to make a quick green sauce, place the lemon juice, capers, herbs, finely chopped walnuts and the remaining oil in a bowl. Season with a pinch of salt and pepper and mix to combine. (Alternatively, blitz the sauce in a blender). Spoon over the vegetables and serve.

PANTRY STAPLES
Canned lentils
Capers
Couscous
Extra-virgin olive oil
Garlic
Ground allspice
Lemon
Onions
Ricotta
Salt and pepper
Walnuts

SHOPPING LIST
Capsicums: green,
    red or yellow
Fresh basil
Fresh flat-leaf
    parsley
Soft goat's cheese

SILVERBEET POLPETTINE

Polpettine is the Italian word for little rissoles or meatballs. The rissoles themselves are delicious, but they're even better wrapped in silverbeet leaves (which is a great way to sneak in extra vegetables!). My dad grows an abundance of silverbeet, so I love to make a big batch of these polpettine and freeze them to have later for a quick weeknight dinner. These also work really well wrapped in Swiss chard or cabbage leaves.

SERVES: 4   PREP: 20 MINUTES   COOK: 45 MINUTES   SUITABLE TO FREEZE

10 large silverbeet leaves, stalks trimmed
1 garlic clove, finely chopped
200 g beef mince
200 g pork mince
1 egg
1 handful of flat-leaf parsley leaves, finely chopped
1 tablespoon raisins, soaked in warm water for 15 minutes to soften, drained
2 tablespoons pine nuts, chopped
95 g (½ cup) leftover cooked long-grain rice, quinoa or couscous
2 large handfuls of freshly grated parmesan or pecorino
salt flakes and freshly ground black pepper
700 g tomato passata
1 tablespoon extra-virgin olive oil
crusty bread, to serve

Preheat the oven to 180°C. Grease a 1.5 litre baking dish.

Bring a large saucepan of salted water to the boil. Add the silverbeet leaves and cook for 3–4 minutes to soften. Drain and pat dry with a clean tea towel. Working with one leaf at a time, lay it out flat and cut the white rib from the centre in a V-shape.

In a large bowl, combine the garlic, beef and pork mince, egg, parsley, raisins, pine nuts, rice, quinoa or couscous and 1 handful of cheese. Season with salt and pepper and combine with your hands.

Divide the mince mixture into ten portions and shape into 10 cm logs. Place each log in the centre of a silverbeet leaf, leaving a small border. Fold in the sides and roll up into a thick sausage-like shape.

Pour half the passata into the prepared dish. Season with salt and pepper, then scatter over a small pinch of cheese and drizzle on half the oil. Nestle in the silverbeet polpettine, seam-side down, then pour over the remaining passata, sprinkle over the remaining cheese and drizzle on the rest of the oil. Bake for 35–40 minutes until the filling is cooked and the sauce is thick and rich. Serve with crusty bread.

PANTRY STAPLES
Beef mince
Crusty bread
Egg
Extra-virgin olive oil
Garlic
Long-grain rice, couscous or quinoa
Parmesan or pecorino
Pine nuts
Pork mince
Raisins
Salt and pepper
Tomato passata

SHOPPING LIST
Fresh flat-leaf parsley
Silverbeet

* To make your own finely crumbled parmesan, rather than grating it, cut a 200 g block of parmesan into chunks and place in a food processor. Pulse eight to ten times until it crumbles. Store in a zip-lock bag in the fridge for 2–3 weeks.

CREAMY PEPPER MUSHROOM TRAY BAKE

I tried a very similar dish to this in a French restaurant recently and thought it was completely wonderful. It's as if you're having a pepper steak with a side of mushroom sauce – but without the steak! And that's my idea of heaven. Leave out the pancetta and it becomes a vegetarian delight that will please everyone. You can absolutely serve these mushrooms as a side to roast beef or chicken, but they're equally delicious as the star, served with a crisp green salad and some crusty bread or even pasta.

SERVES: 4   PREP: 15 MINUTES   COOK: 25 MINUTES

600 g field mushrooms, brushed
   and stalks trimmed
2 tablespoons extra-virgin olive oil
salt flakes
1 x 100 g piece of flat pancetta,
   cut into lardons
1 French shallot, finely chopped
2 garlic cloves, chopped
3 tablespoons port or sherry
2 tablespoons green peppercorns
   in brine, drained and crushed
125 ml (½ cup) chicken stock
100 ml cream
50 g hazelnuts, skins removed,
   roughly chopped
1 small handful of flat-leaf parsley
   leaves, finely chopped

Preheat the oven to 200°C.

Tightly place the mushrooms in a single layer in a baking dish (it's okay if they overlap a little as they will shrink significantly). Drizzle over 1 tablespoon of oil, season with a pinch of salt and bake for 10–12 minutes until the mushrooms start to soften.

Meanwhile, heat the remaining oil in a saucepan over medium–low heat and add the pancetta, shallot and garlic. Gently cook, stirring regularly to allow the fat to render from the pancetta, for 3–4 minutes until the shallot and garlic are softened and lightly caramelised. Pour in the port or sherry and stir to deglaze the pan. Add the peppercorns and stock and simmer until reduced by one-third. Pour in the cream and cook for a further 2–3 minutes until slightly thickened.

Drain most of the excess liquid from the mushrooms, then pour over the cream sauce and sprinkle on the hazelnuts. Bake for a further 10–12 minutes until the mushrooms are tender. Sprinkle over the parsley and serve.

 Use bacon or speck instead of pancetta, if you like.

PANTRY STAPLES
Chicken stock
Cream
Extra-virgin olive oil
French shallot
Garlic
Green peppercorns
Hazelnuts
Port or sherry
Salt

SHOPPING LIST
Field mushrooms
Fresh flat-leaf
   parsley
Pancetta

SWEET POTATO JACKETS WITH CHORIZO

These chorizo-filled jackets are a great twist on the traditional potato version.
I love the balance of the sweetness from the sweet potato and the punchy
robust flavour from the chorizo and vinegar.

SERVES: 4   PREP: 15 MINUTES   COOK: 1 HOUR 10 MINUTES

4 small sweet potatoes (each about
    300 g), unpeeled
1 red onion, finely sliced into rings
2 tablespoons sherry vinegar
    (or balsamic or red wine vinegar)
salt flakes and freshly ground
    black pepper
1 tablespoon olive oil
2 chorizo sausages, casings
    removed, torn into small pieces
    (alternatively, coarsely chop in
    a food processor)
1 garlic clove, chopped
1 teaspoon smoked paprika
100 g cheddar, coarsely grated
2 tablespoons natural yoghurt
    or sour cream

Preheat the oven to 180°C. Line a baking tray with baking paper.

Place the sweet potatoes on the prepared tray and bake for 45–55 minutes until the skins are slightly dry and crisp and the flesh inside is just tender when pierced with a knife. Cool for 5 minutes.

Combine the red onion with 1 tablespoon of vinegar and a pinch of salt and set aside to lightly pickle.

Meanwhile, place the oil and chorizo in a frying pan over low heat and cook for 2 minutes, gradually increasing the heat to medium (this renders the fat and creates crispy chorizo). Cook for a further 4–5 minutes, frequently tossing, until the chorizo is crunchy. Stir in the garlic and paprika and cook for 30 seconds, then add the remaining vinegar, stir to deglaze the pan and remove from the heat.

Cut a slit lengthways down the centre of each sweet potato, being careful to go only three-quarters of the way through. With a dessertspoon and trying not to pierce the skins, scoop out 2–3 tablespoons of flesh to create a cavity. Mix the flesh with the chorizo mixture. Return the hollowed-out skins to the baking tray.

Add one-third of the cheese to the chorizo mixture and check the seasoning – it may need a small pinch of salt and pepper. Mix with a fork, then evenly divide the mixture among the sweet potato skins and sprinkle over the remaining cheese. Bake for 10–15 minutes until the cheese is bubbly and melted.

Dollop the yoghurt or sour cream on the sweet potato jackets, sprinkle over the pickled onion and serve.

PANTRY STAPLES   SHOPPING LIST

Cheddar
Chorizo sausages
Garlic
Olive oil
Red onion
Salt and pepper
Smoked paprika
Sweet potatoes
Vinegar (sherry, red
    wine or balsamic)
Yoghurt or
    sour cream

BROCCOLI, PEA AND CHEDDAR TART

If using frozen square shortcrust pastry from the supermarket for this tart, use two thawed sheets. Lay the first sheet over half the tin and press into the base and sides. Place the other piece of pastry on the other side and join by pressing along the centre with a fork (just like patchwork). Cut away the excess pastry from the sides with a small sharp knife.

SERVES: 6   PREP: 15 MINUTES   COOK: 1 HOUR

butter, for greasing
1 head of broccoli (about 200 g),
   cut into florets
65 g (½ cup) frozen baby peas
445 g frozen shortcrust pastry
   (or make my pastry recipe on
   page 192), thawed
6 eggs
500 ml (2 cups) pure or thickened
   cream
pinch of freshly grated nutmeg
salt flakes and freshly ground
   black pepper
60 g cheddar, coarsely grated
20 g parmesan, finely grated

Preheat the oven to 180°C. Grease a 30 cm x 20 cm rectangular tart tin and line with baking paper.

Bring a large saucepan of water to the boil and add the broccoli. When the water comes back to the boil, add the peas and cook for 1 minute. Drain and pat dry with paper towel.

Roll out the pastry between two sheets of baking paper to form a 2–3 mm thick rectangle that will cover the base and sides of the tart tin. Place the pastry in the tin, ensuring there are no air bubbles, and trim the excess pastry with a small sharp knife. Prick the pasty with a fork and line with a piece of baking paper. Fill with baking weights, dried beans or uncooked rice and blind-bake for 15 minutes. Remove from the oven and carefully remove the baking paper and weights, then return to the oven and bake for a further 5 minutes until the pastry is dry and lightly golden. Set aside to cool a little.

Whisk the eggs with the cream and add the nutmeg, salt and pepper.

Place the tart shell on a baking tray and scatter the broccoli and peas over the base. Sprinkle the cheeses over the vegetables, then carefully pour on the cream mixture. Return the tart to the oven on the lowest shelf (this helps to crisp the base). Bake for 30–35 minutes until the tart is puffed and golden with a very slight wobble in the centre. Serve warm or cold.

PANTRY STAPLES
Butter
Cheddar
Cream
Eggs
Frozen baby peas
Frozen shortcrust
   pastry
Nutmeg
Parmesan
Salt and pepper

SHOPPING LIST
Broccoli

SILKY EGGPLANT AND PRAWN PARCELS

Cooking en papillote (baked in a parcel) is a wonderful technique to learn. The food is insulated because it's tightly wrapped in baking paper, keeping it moist and allowing the flavours to mingle in the steam, making it super flavoursome. The best bit is bringing the parcels to the table. When you pierce them open, a cloud of fragrant steam wafts out, bringing with it a sense of drama and a wonderful element of surprise.

SERVES: 4   PREP: 15 MINUTES   COOK: 35 MINUTES

2 eggplants (about 600 g), peeled and cut into 3 cm pieces
125 ml (½ cup) chicken stock
1½ teaspoons sesame oil
2 tablespoons soy sauce, plus extra to serve
1 tablespoon shaoxing wine
1 tablespoon chilli paste (such as sambal oelek or harissa)
1 heaped teaspoon caster sugar
300 g silken tofu, drained and pressed dry with paper towel, cut into 4 pieces
12 raw large prawns, shelled and deveined with tails intact
salt flakes
toasted sesame seeds, to serve
6 spring onions, finely julienned (see Note)

Preheat the oven to 180°C.

Place the eggplant and chicken stock in a microwave-safe bowl, cover with plastic wrap and microwave for 10–12 minutes until the eggplant is soft. Stand, covered, until required. Alternatively, place the eggplant in a steamer basket over a saucepan of simmering water, cover and steam for 10–12 minutes until softened, then add to a bowl and pour in the stock.

Combine the sesame oil, soy sauce, shaoxing wine, chilli paste and sugar in a bowl and whisk together. Pour over the eggplant mixture, add the tofu and gently stir through, breaking up the tofu slightly.

Layer two 30 cm square sheets of baking paper over a 500 ml bowl, making sure the corners sit up to contain the liquid. Spoon on 1 cup of the eggplant mixture and top with three prawns and a sprinkle of salt. Bring the corners together, scrunch to form a parcel and tie with a piece of kitchen string. Repeat this process with the remaining eggplant mixture and prawns to make four parcels in total. Place on a baking tray and bake for 15–20 minutes until the prawns are cooked through.

To serve, transfer the parcels to serving bowls, open and sprinkle over the sesame seeds and spring onion. Serve with extra soy sauce on the side.

* To julienne the spring onions, cut into 10 cm batons, then cut in half horizontally. Finely slice into thin strips. To make them curl, place the strips in a bowl of iced water for 10 minutes.

PANTRY STAPLES
Caster sugar
Chicken stock
Chilli paste
Salt
Sesame oil
Sesame seeds
Shaoxing wine
Silken tofu
Soy sauce

SHOPPING LIST
Eggplants
Prawns
Spring onions

MADRAS FISH PILAF

In this recipe, I've tried to mirror the way a slow-cooked meat biryani is cooked, but instead of using meat, I've cut the cooking time in half by using fish and a store-bought curry paste. I love it when I bring this dish to the table, as my guests are pleasantly surprised that under the fluffy white rice layer is a fragrant fish curry.

SERVES: 4   PREP: 10 MINUTES   COOK: 1 HOUR 15 MINUTES

2 tablespoons vegetable oil
1 onion, finely sliced
3 cm piece of ginger, finely chopped
3 tablespoons Madras curry paste
1 x 400 g can whole peeled
   tomatoes, drained
1 x 400 ml can coconut milk
250 g frozen spinach, thawed
300 g (1 ½ cups) basmati rice
2 cardamom pods, crushed
1 fresh bay leaf
salt flakes
700 g blue-eye trevalla fillets
   (or kingfish, swordfish, blue
   grenadier or salmon), skin
   removed and pin-boned,
   cut into 5 cm chunks
20 g (¼ cup) crispy fried shallots
mango chutney, to serve

Heat the oil in a 3 litre flameproof casserole dish over medium heat. Add the onion and cook for 3–4 minutes to soften and caramelise before adding the ginger. Stir regularly for 2 minutes, then add the curry paste and cook for a minute until fragrant. Tip in the tomatoes and break up with a wooden spoon, then pour in the coconut milk. Increase the heat to high and bring to the boil. Cook, stirring regularly so the sauce doesn't catch, for 10 minutes until thickened. Add the spinach and cook for a further 5 minutes until the sauce is thick enough to coat the back of a spoon. Remove from the heat and cool for 10–15 minutes.

Preheat the oven to 180°C.

Rinse the rice three or four times in cold water until the water runs clear. Pour 1 litre of water into a large saucepan, add the cardamom and bay leaf and bring to the boil. Add the rice and a pinch of salt and cook for 5–8 minutes until al dente. Drain, reserving the cardamom and bay leaf to flavour the rice while it cooks in the oven.

Place the fish in the sauce and fold through. Top with the rice, spread out evenly with the back of a spoon and sprinkle on 3 tablespoons of water to ensure the rice steams and stays moist. Cover with foil and a tight-fitting lid and bake for 40 minutes until the rice is cooked. Scatter over the crispy fried shallots and serve with some mango chutney on the side.

PANTRY STAPLES
Basmati rice
Bay leaf
Canned whole
  peeled tomatoes
Cardamom pods
Coconut milk
Crispy fried shallots
Fresh ginger
Frozen spinach
Madras curry paste
Onion
Salt
Vegetable oil

SHOPPING LIST
Mango chutney
White fish fillets

* Crispy fried shallots can be found in the Asian aisle of your supermarket. Another lovely alternative for a slight textural contrast is lightly toasted desiccated coconut.

Mango chutney can be found in the Asian and Indian section of the supermarket.

If you feel like a change from fish fillets, fish cutlets are a great option. This cut is like a fish steak with the centre bone still attached. I like to use cutlets when my fishmonger has them, as the bone keeps the fish incredibly moist.

The madras curry paste can be swapped for goan, tikka masala or korma curry paste, if you like.

GO-TO SAUCES & DRESSINGS

1. Splash some vegetable oil into a saucepan and add 2 tablespoons of Thai curry paste. Cook over medium heat for 2–3 minutes until aromatic. Add 1 teaspoon of sugar, a splash of fish sauce and 270 ml of coconut milk and bring to the boil. Cook until thick enough to coat the back of a spoon. Remove from the heat. Squeeze in the juice of 1 lime. Serve with grilled chicken or schnitzel or drizzle over steamed Asian greens.

2. For my go-to salad dressing, combine 1 heaped teaspoon of dijon mustard, 1 tablespoon of vinegar of your choice and a pinch of salt and pepper in a salad bowl. While constantly whisking, drizzle in 80 ml of olive oil until emulsified. Just before serving (to ensure the leaves stay crisp), throw in a few large handfuls of lettuce leaves and toss. Perfect for any salad, this is also great simply drizzled into avocado cavities for a quick lunch or entrée.

3. For a citrus and ginger dressing, whisk together 1 teaspoon of grated ginger, the juice of 1 orange and 1 tablespoon of soy sauce. In a slow and steady stream, pour in 80 ml (⅓ cup) of olive oil, whisking until combined. Delicious with a cold soba noodle salad.

4. Jazz up your classic chicken sandwich by combining 2 tablespoons of whole-egg mayonnaise, 2 tablespoons of natural yoghurt, a small squeeze of lemon juice and a teaspoon of curry powder. Shred the chicken and fold into the curried mayonnaise.

5. Gribiche, a classic French sauce, is great with cold leftover meat, steamed fennel and asparagus, grilled, battered or fried fish or as a dressing for potato salad. Mix 125 g (½ cup) of whole-egg mayonnaise with 1 teaspoon of dijon mustard, a mashed soft-boiled egg, a small handful of finely chopped flat-leaf parsley, chervil and tarragon leaves, and a small handul of chopped cornichons, capers and French shallot.

6. For a super-quick chimichurri, pound 1 garlic clove, 1 small red chilli and a pinch each of salt, dried oregano and smoked paprika using a mortar and pestle. Add a large handful of flat-leaf parsley and coriander leaves and pound to a rough paste. Pour in 80 ml (⅓ cup) of olive oil and mix through. Serve with your favourite barbecued meat.

7. For a silky avocado sauce, place 2 peeled and stoned avocados, 3 tablespoons of Greek yoghurt, the juice of ½ lemon and 1 tablespoon of tahini in a blender and season with a pinch of salt. Blend until smooth. Serve with grilled salmon, dusted with toasted sesame seeds. It's also super tasty with couscous or quinoa and spinach.

8. Onion jam is simple. Fry 2 finely sliced onions in butter and olive oil over medium heat for 8–10 minutes until softened. Deglaze the pan with 3 tablespoons of beer of your choice. Add 1 teaspoon of sugar and 2 tablespoons of balsamic vinegar and simmer until thick and sticky. Serve alongside steaks or add to a steak sandwich.

TUNA MOUSSAKA

This is a great dish to prepare when you have vegetables left over from a roast dinner. You can replace the eggplant and potato with pumpkin, sweet potato, parsnip, cauliflower or broccoli. All you need do is roughly chop the veggies and place half on the base and half on top of the tuna sauce. I sometimes incorporate leftover lentils into the tuna sauce to bulk it out a little.

To make this vegetarian, replace the tuna with two 400 gram cans of mixed beans or lentils.

SERVES: 6   **PREP:** 20 MINUTES   **COOK:** 1 HOUR 15 MINUTES   **SUITABLE TO FREEZE**

4 desiree potatoes (about 700 g),
   cut into 1 cm thick rounds
1 eggplant, cut into 1 cm thick rounds
3 tablespoons extra-virgin olive oil,
   plus extra for greasing
salt flakes
2 onions, finely chopped
3 garlic cloves, finely chopped
½ teaspoon ground cloves
1 teaspoon dried oregano
2 x 400 g cans whole peeled
   tomatoes, juices drained
   from 1 can
freshly ground black pepper
1 x 425 g can tuna in spring
   water, drained

CHEESE SAUCE
60 g butter
60 g plain flour, plus extra for dusting
700 ml milk
salt flakes
200 g kefalograviera cheese

Preheat the oven to 180°C. Line two large baking trays with foil and then baking paper (this makes washing up easier).

Arrange the potato and eggplant on the prepared trays in a single layer and drizzle with half the oil. Season the vegetables with salt and bake for 15–20 minutes until tender and golden brown.

Heat the remaining oil in a sauté pan over medium heat and add the onion and garlic. Cook, stirring regularly, for 4–5 minutes until softened. Add the cloves, dried oregano and tomatoes, season with salt and pepper and, using a wooden spoon, crush the tomatoes to break them up. Bring to the boil and cook for 15 minutes until thick and rich. Add the tuna and break it up a little with a fork, then cook for a further minute to warm through.

Meanwhile, for the cheese sauce, melt the butter in a saucepan over medium heat, add the flour and cook, stirring constantly, for 2 minutes until the roux is golden and combined. Gradually whisk in the milk and cook, whisking constantly, for 3 minutes until the sauce becomes thick and glossy. Remove from the heat, season with salt and stir in half the cheese.

To assemble, grease a 3 litre baking dish with a little oil and cover the base with a layer of potato followed by a layer of eggplant. Add the tuna sauce and spread out to completely cover the eggplant. Add another layer of potato, then a layer of eggplant and top evenly with the cheese sauce. Sprinkle over the remaining cheese and bake for 30–35 minutes until golden brown.

 You can use cheddar or parmesan instead of kefalograviera cheese, if you like.

PANTRY STAPLES	SHOPPING LIST
Butter	Eggplant
Canned tuna in	Kefalograviera
spring water	cheese
Canned whole	
peeled tomatoes	
Desiree potatoes	
Dried oregano	
Extra-virgin olive oil	
Garlic	
Ground cloves	
Milk	
Onions	
Plain flour	
Salt and pepper	

CRISPY SALMON WITH JAPANESE 'PANTRY SAUCE'

I make this dish at least once a week, not only because it's super quick and I always have the marinade ingredients on hand, but also because you get an incredible textural result with the fish – crispy 'crackling' skin and moist melt-in-your-mouth fillets. Serve with steamed rice and Asian greens or, for a quick and healthy side, add a generous spoonful of fermented vegetables, such as kimchi, which I love to keep in the fridge.

SERVES: 4   PREP: 10 MINUTES, PLUS 20 MINUTES MARINATING   COOK: 15 MINUTES

vegetable oil, for brushing
4 x 200 g centre-cut salmon fillets,
    skin on, pin-boned

MARINADE

2 tablespoons white (shiro)
    miso paste
3 tablespoons soy sauce
2 tablespoons sake or
    shaoxing wine
2 tablespoons honey
2 cm piece of ginger, grated

Preheat the grill element in the oven. Line a baking tray with foil and fit a wire rack on top, then brush the rack with the oil. Cooking the fish on the rack will ensure it cooks evenly and doesn't stick.

To make the marinade, whisk all the ingredients together in a shallow dish.

Place the fish, flesh-side down, in the marinade, ensuring the skin doesn't get too much marinade on it. This will prevent the skin from charring too much. Cover and marinate at room temperature for 15–20 minutes.

Working with one piece of fish at a time, wipe the excess marinade off. Arrange the fish, skin-side up, on the prepared rack and slide onto the middle rack in the oven. Grill for 7–12 minutes until the skin blisters and chars slightly (this imparts a lovely smoky flavour).

Meanwhile, place the remaining marinade in a small saucepan, bring to the boil and cook for 2 minutes. Remove from the heat, brush over the fish and serve any leftover marinade on the side.

 Every oven grill is different, so keep a close eye on the fish as it grills. If the skin is darkening too quickly, simply move the tray to a lower shelf in the oven.

PANTRY STAPLES

Fresh ginger
Honey
Miso paste
Sake or shaoxing
    wine
Soy sauce
Vegetable oil

SHOPPING LIST

Salmon fillets

YOGHURT-CRUSTED CHICKEN STRIPS

This no-fuss dish is the epitome of a quick weeknight family dinner. I use a traditional supermarket curry powder that is mild in flavour so the kids will love it. I do say to marinate the chicken for at least an hour to allow the flavours to penetrate better and tenderise the chicken, but this is not crucial; the results are just as delicious if you cook the chicken strips immediately after coating in the yoghurt sauce.

SERVES: 4   **PREP:** 15 MINUTES, PLUS 1 HOUR MARINATING   **COOK:** 25 MINUTES

400 g Greek yoghurt
125 ml (½ cup) coconut cream
1 onion, finely chopped
1 garlic clove, finely chopped
1 ½ tablespoons mild curry powder
4 chicken breast fillets (about 1 kg)
salt flakes and freshly ground
   black pepper
2 teaspoons cumin seeds

PANTRY STAPLES
Coconut cream
Cumin seeds
Curry powder
Garlic
Greek yoghurt
Onion
Salt and pepper

SHOPPING LIST
Chicken breast
fillets

Combine the yoghurt, coconut cream, onion, garlic and curry powder in a large glass or ceramic bowl.

Cut each chicken breast in half lengthways so you have eight strips, then place the chicken in the marinade, add a generous pinch of salt and pepper and mix to combine. Cover with plastic wrap and transfer to the fridge to marinate for 1 hour, or even better overnight.

Preheat the oven to 210°C. Line a large baking tray with foil and then baking paper.

Remove the chicken strips from the marinade, allowing the excess marinade to drip back into the bowl. Place the chicken on the prepared tray, leaving a little space between each strip. Bake for 15 minutes until the chicken starts to form a crispy charred crust.

Meanwhile, place the remaining marinade in a small saucepan and bring to the boil. Cook for 2–3 minutes until thickened. Generously brush over the chicken, sprinkle on the cumin seeds and bake for a further 10 minutes.

BARRAMUNDI FILLETS WITH ROASTED FENNEL

Fennel is delicious roasted and it's particularly good when paired with fish. Here, the sweet anise flavour of the fennel perfumes the fish and the coriander seeds impart a lovely citrus note, which creates, without trying too hard, quite an elegant dinner. This simple recipe is all about timing, so ensure the fennel is roasted until tender before adding the fish fillets, as they don't take long to cook.

SERVES: 4   PREP: 10 MINUTES   COOK: 55 MINUTES

1 heaped teaspoon coriander seeds
2 garlic cloves, peeled
salt flakes
3 tablespoons extra-virgin olive oil
2 fennel bulbs, cut into 1.5 cm thick
   wedges, fronds reserved
160 ml white wine (such as
   chardonnay or sauvignon blanc)
4 x 180 g barramundi fillets
   (or other white fish such as
   blue-eye trevalla, blue grenadier
   or snapper), skin on, pin-boned
20 g butter, cubed
250 g cherry truss tomatoes

Preheat the oven to 200°C.

Using a mortar and pestle, lightly crush the coriander seeds, then add the garlic and a pinch of salt and crush to form a sticky paste. Stir in 2 tablespoons of oil.

Place the fennel wedges in a large deep baking tray. Drizzle over the coriander oil and massage into the fennel with your hands, then pour on the wine and bake for 40 minutes until tender.

Coat the fish in the remaining olive oil and season with salt. Remove the baking tray from the oven, toss and arrange the fish on the fennel. Add the butter and tomatoes and return to the oven for 10–12 minutes until the fish is cooked through and the fennel is caramelised. Scatter over the reserved fennel fronds and serve.

PANTRY STAPLES

Butter
Coriander seeds
Extra-virgin olive oil
Garlic
Salt
White wine

SHOPPING LIST

Barramundi fillets
Cherry truss
   tomatoes
Fennel bulbs

* If you'd like to bulk out this dish, add halved new potatoes when you roast the fennel.

GREEK CHICKEN AND PEAS

This is one of those recipes where the oven does all the work. Using chicken thighs on the bone (drumsticks are a great substitute) keeps the chicken moist and gives the peas and pan juices a lovely flavour. If you want to speed up the process, chicken thigh fillets also work nicely – simply reduce the cooking time by 10 minutes. For a different complexity, substitute white wine for the lemon juice. And for an extra-rich sauce, add a 400 gram can of drained and crushed whole peeled tomatoes to the peas and potato.

SERVES: 4–6   PREP: 10 MINUTES   COOK: 1 HOUR 5 MINUTES

500 g frozen baby peas

500 g waxy new potatoes (such as kipfler, Dutch cream or desiree), peeled and halved (or quartered if large)

2 tomatoes, quartered

juice of 1 large lemon

1 ½ teaspoons dried oregano

250 ml (1 cup) chicken stock

3 tablespoons extra-virgin olive oil

salt flakes and freshly ground black pepper

6 chicken thighs, skin on and bone in

Preheat the oven to 200°C.

Place the peas, potato, tomato, lemon juice, oregano, stock and 1 ½ tablespoons of oil in a 3 litre baking dish and season with salt and pepper. Mix to ensure the peas and potato are scattered evenly. Bake for 25 minutes.

Drizzle the remaining oil over the chicken and season with salt and pepper. Remove the tray from the oven and arrange the chicken, skin-side up, on top of the pea mixture. Bake for 20 minutes to create a lovely crust on the chicken. Give the dish a quick shake and cook for a further 15–20 minutes until the chicken is cooked through and the skin is crispy and blistered on top and the peas and potato are soft, sticky and caramelised.

PANTRY STAPLES

Chicken stock
Dried oregano
Extra-virgin olive oil
Frozen baby peas
Lemon
Salt and pepper

SHOPPING LIST

Chicken thighs
Tomatoes
Waxy new potatoes

BUTTERFLIED CHICKEN WITH QUICK CAPSICUM SALSA

Roasting a butterflied chicken cuts cooking time and makes the idea of enjoying a mid-week roast appealing. You can get your butcher to butterfly the bird, but if you want to have a go yourself it's actually very easy. Place the chicken, breast-side down, on a chopping board and, using sharp kitchen scissors or a knife, cut down either side of the backbone and remove and discard (or save for stock). Turn the chicken over and use the palm of your hand to press down on the chicken and flatten. Serve with roasted spuds (see page 25).

SERVES: 4 **PREP:** 20 MINUTES **COOK:** 50 MINUTES, PLUS 15 MINUTES RESTING

1 x 1.8 kg chicken, butterflied
(ask your butcher to do this
or see instructions above)
1 garlic bulb, halved horizontally
2 cm piece of ginger, sliced
300 g jarred roasted red capsicum,
drained and roughly chopped
125 ml (½ cup) olive oil
salt flakes and freshly ground
black pepper
100 ml red wine vinegar
1 tablespoon caster sugar
1 tablespoon chilli paste
(such as sambal oelek or harissa)
1 small handful of flat-leaf
parsley leaves

Remove the chicken from the fridge 1 hour before cooking.

Preheat the oven to 210°C.

Scatter the garlic, ginger and capsicum into a roasting tin.

Place the chicken, skin-side up, in the tin, ensuring the garlic, ginger and capsicum are under the chicken so they do not burn. Drizzle 1 tablespoon of oil over the chicken and season with salt and pepper. Roast for 35–45 minutes until the chicken is crisp and lightly charred. Transfer the chicken to a plate, reserve the roasted veggies, and rest in a warm place for 10–15 minutes.

Meanwhile, place the vinegar and sugar in a saucepan, bring to the boil and cook until the sugar has dissolved.

Squeeze half the softened garlic flesh into the bowl of a small food processor (keep the other half for serving, if you like) and add the roasted ginger, chilli paste and vinegar mixture. Blend until smooth, then slowly blend in the remaining oil to form a thick sauce. Now add the roast capsicum and pulse four or five times until well combined but still a little chunky. Check for seasoning.

Spoon the capsicum salsa over the chicken and serve with the parsley and the remaining garlic, if desired.

PANTRY STAPLES
Caster sugar
Chilli paste
Fresh ginger
Garlic
Jarred roasted red
capsicum
Olive oil
Red wine vinegar
Salt and pepper

SHOPPING LIST
Fresh flat-leaf
parsley
Whole chicken

✳ This is also a great recipe for the barbecue. Simply cook the chicken over medium heat for 15–20 minutes on each side, turning four times throughout the cooking process. Meanwhile, briefly cook the ginger and garlic on the barbecue to get some colour, then wrap in foil to steam. The capsicum simply needs to char for 2 minutes on each side, then make the salsa as above.

RED CURRY CHICKEN TRAY BAKE

Tray bakes – like this Thai-inspired version – have evolved from many traditional dishes. I've cut some corners here to cook everything in one tray, and I'm unapologetic about it because the results are superb and there are fewer dishes to clean up! Using only a handful of good-quality pantry staples, such as curry paste, fish sauce and coconut milk, you can create a delicious sauce for the chicken drumsticks. I love a pop of sweetness with this, so I've added canned pineapple. Canned lychees working well, too. Serve with steamed rice and Asian greens.

SERVES: 4   PREP: 10 MINUTES   COOK: 35 MINUTES

1 x 400 ml can coconut milk
3 tablespoons red curry paste
1 tablespoon fish sauce
1 onion, sliced
225 g canned pineapple slices, drained and quartered
8 chicken drumsticks
juice of ½ lime
50 g (⅓ cup) unsalted cashew nuts, lightly toasted and roughly chopped
1 small handful of coriander leaves

Preheat the oven to 180°C.

Whisk the coconut milk into the curry paste, then add the fish sauce. Pour into a 2 litre baking dish, then scatter over the onion and pineapple. Using tongs, coat the chicken in the sauce, then nestle the drumsticks in the dish in a single layer. Bake for 30–35 minutes until the chicken is cooked through and the skin is crisp and blistered and the sauce is thick and rich. Give the dish a little shake halfway through to ensure the onion and pineapple don't stick.

Squeeze the lime juice over the chicken and scatter on the cashew nuts and coriander.

PANTRY STAPLES
Canned pineapple slices
Cashew nuts
Coconut milk
Fish sauce
Onion
Red curry paste

SHOPPING LIST
Chicken drumsticks
Fresh coriander
Lime

* Other jarred curry pastes, such as green, yellow or Massaman, work well with this recipe, too. It's also delicious with Indian curry pastes, such as butter chicken, korma etc.

STICKY GLAZED GINGER CHICKEN

With its glistening glaze, this sticky chicken is one of my hero weeknight dishes. Everyone I make this for wants the recipe. If you can, use chicken thigh on the bone for the most succulent results. The most appealing thing about this dish is that you can whip it up with classic pantry ingredients. Add this one to your repertoire – it will never disappoint.

SERVES: 4–6   **PREP:** 10 MINUTES   **COOK:** 1 HOUR

8 chicken thighs, skin on
  and bone in

GLAZE

140 g (¾ cup) brown sugar
1 teaspoon ground ginger
3 tablespoons soy sauce
3 tablespoons red wine vinegar
2 tablespoons dijon mustard
1 teaspoon tomato paste

Preheat the oven to 180°C. Line a baking tray with foil and then baking paper, then place a wire rack on top. (The glaze is sticky, so this step is worth doing to make light work of washing up later.)

To make the glaze, combine all the ingredients in a small saucepan, whisk and bring to the boil. Reduce the heat to low and cook for 5–8 minutes until the glaze is glossy and coats the back of a spoon.

Brush some of the glaze over the chicken and bake, basting every 10 minutes with the remaining glaze, for 40–45 minutes until the chicken is cooked through and the skin is blistered with a lovely glossy crust.

PANTRY STAPLES	**SHOPPING LIST**
Brown sugar	Chicken thighs
Dijon mustard	
Ground ginger	
Red wine vinegar	
Soy sauce	
Tomato paste	

✱ You can also use chicken drumsticks, boneless chicken thighs or a whole chicken cut into eight pieces.

For the ultimate crispy skin, air-dry the chicken pieces overnight in the fridge – sit them uncovered on a wire rack.

MEATLOAF IN SMOKY BARBECUE SAUCE

I love to make traditional home-style American meatloaf, because most of the ingredients are staples I have in my fridge and pantry – and you probably do, too. I've tested a few different versions over the years, but this one is by far my top pick: it perfectly balances the smokiness from the bacon (which also protects the meat while it's cooking, keeping it super moist) with the sticky sweet and sour sauce. This meatloaf is best served with a simple slaw and/or baked potatoes. And leftovers are fantastic, particularly as a sandwich filler.

SERVES: 4   PREP: 15 MINUTES   COOK: 1 HOUR   SUITABLE TO FREEZE

1 tablespoon olive oil, plus extra
    for greasing
1 onion, finely chopped
1 carrot, finely grated
150 ml apple cider vinegar
200 ml hoisin sauce
200 g tomato passata
1 teaspoon Chinese five spice
500 g beef mince
salt flakes and freshly ground
    black pepper
1 teaspoon dried oregano
50 g cheddar, coarsely grated
1 egg
2 handfuls of fresh breadcrumbs
8 streaky bacon rashers

Preheat the oven to 180°C. Line a tray with baking paper and brush with a little oil.

Heat the oil in a sauté pan over medium heat, add the onion and carrot and cook for 4–5 minutes to soften. Remove from the heat, place in a large bowl and cool to room temperature.

Meanwhile, wipe the pan clean and add the vinegar, hoisin sauce, tomato passata and Chinese five spice. Pour in 125 ml (½ cup) of water and bring to a gentle boil. Simmer for 5–10 minutes until the sauce is thick and fragrant. Remove the pan from the heat and cover with a lid.

Place the mince in the bowl with the onion mixture. Season with salt and pepper and add the dried oregano, cheese, egg, breadcrumbs and 1 tablespoon of the sauce. Using your hands, mix everything together. Shape into a log about 20 cm long and brush with a little sauce. Lay the bacon down on the baking tray with the slices overlapping. Top with the log of meat, then wrap the bacon around to enclose the meat. Flip over and place, seam-side down, on the tray. Brush the meatloaf with more sauce and bake for 40–45 minutes until cooked through, basting every 15 minutes. Remove from the oven, cool for 5 minutes, then baste with more sauce.

Reheat the remaining sauce and serve alongside the meatloaf.

PANTRY STAPLES   SHOPPING LIST

Apple cider vinegar
Bacon
Beef mince
Carrot
Cheddar
Chinese five spice
Dried oregano
Egg
Fresh breadcrumbs
Hoisin sauce
Olive oil
Onion
Salt and pepper
Tomato passata

TORTILLA PIES

This is such a fun way to transform the classic taco. I took inspiration for this recipe from a fast-food outlet in America (of all places). It's a 'surprise' taco, as the yummy filling is encased in a soft tortilla wrap then toasted to create a crusty outer casing – when you cut into it, you get the satisfaction of all your favourite taco fillings. To freeze, make the pies and freeze on a tray. Thaw in the fridge for a few hours, then warm through in the oven at 180°C for 20 minutes.

SERVES: 6   **PREP:** 20 MINUTES   **COOK:** 45 MINUTES, PLUS 10 MINUTES COOLING
SUITABLE TO FREEZE

2 tablespoons olive oil,
   plus extra for brushing
1 red onion, finely diced
1 red capsicum, diced
1 garlic clove, chopped
1 teaspoon smoked paprika
½ teaspoon ground cumin
½ teaspoon ground coriander
300 g beef mince
salt flakes and freshly ground
   black pepper
200 g canned kidney beans,
   drained and rinsed
1 x 400 g can whole peeled
   tomatoes, crushed
8 large flour tortillas
3 tablespoons sour cream
60 g (½ cup) grated cheddar,
   plus extra to serve

SALSA
½ red onion, finely sliced
grated zest and juice of ½ lime
1 avocado, diced
1 long green chilli, finely sliced

Heat the oil in a sauté pan over medium heat. Add the onion, capsicum and garlic and cook for 3–4 minutes until softened. Stir in the spices and cook for 1 minute more. Add the mince, break up any lumps with a fork and season with salt and pepper. Cook for 2 minutes, then add the beans and tomatoes. Cover and cook, stirring occasionally, for 15–20 minutes until the sauce is thick and rich. Set aside to cool for 10 minutes.

Preheat the oven to 180°C.

Using a 5 cm round cookie cutter, cut out six discs from two tortillas and set aside. Place the remaining tortillas on a work surface and spread 2 teaspoons of sour cream in the centre of each. Add about ½ cup of meat sauce to each and sprinkle with the cheese. Top each with a 5 cm disc, then fold in the sides to enclose the filling.

Brush the tortilla pies with a little oil. Arrange, seam-side down, on a large baking tray and bake for 10–15 minutes until lightly toasted and warmed through.

For the salsa, combine the onion, lime zest and juice and a pinch of salt in a bowl. Marinate for 5 minutes before mixing in the avocado and chilli.

Spoon the salsa over each hot tortilla pie and serve with the salsa and a little extra cheese.

* The meat sauce can be prepared up to 3 days ahead. I like to make a big batch (simply double the recipe) and freeze one portion to have on standby for a quick weeknight dinner.

This recipe also works well with other fillings, such as leftover bolognese or meat and vegetable stews.

To make the tortillas more pliable, warm them in the microwave for 30 seconds before using.

PANTRY STAPLES
Beef mince
Canned kidney beans
Canned whole
   peeled tomatoes
Cheddar
Flour tortillas
Garlic
Ground coriander
Ground cumin
Olive oil
Red onions
Salt and pepper
Smoked paprika
Sour cream

SHOPPING LIST
Avocado
Fresh long green
   chilli
Lime
Red capsicum

STOVETOP

SPLIT PEA AND CAULIFLOWER CURRY

Essentially this is a dhal, but I've put my own stamp on it by bulking it out with cauliflower. There are hundreds of different regional variations of dhal. I use coconut milk in mine, so it's similar to a Sri Lankan version. Dhal can be made with a variety of pulses, not just lentils, so I've added split peas as they give a beautiful creamy result. Serve as is or as a side to a curry banquet.

SERVES: 4   PREP: 10 MINUTES   COOK: 35 MINUTES

200 g (1 cup) yellow split peas
1 onion, chopped
salt flakes
½ head of cauliflower (350–400 g),
   cut into small florets
270 ml canned coconut milk,
   plus extra to serve, if desired
2 tablespoons coconut oil
1½ teaspoons ground turmeric
2 teaspoons cumin seeds
1 small green chilli, finely chopped
3 tablespoons crispy fried shallots
1 small handful of mint leaves

Place the split peas and onion in a large saucepan and cover with 1.5 litres of water. Add a good pinch of salt and bring to the boil, skimming off the impurities that rise to the surface. Reduce the heat and simmer for 15 minutes. Add the cauliflower and continue to cook for a further 15 minutes until the split peas are tender. Stir in the coconut milk and cook for 2 minutes until the curry has thickened.

Heat the coconut oil in a small frying pan over medium heat and add the turmeric, cumin seeds and most of the chilli. Cook for a few seconds until fragrant, then tip into the curry. Fold through, then check the seasoning and remove the curry from the heat. Scatter on the fried shallots, mint leaves and reserved chilli and serve drizzled with a little extra coconut milk, if you like.

 Serve with the flatbread on page 15 or some good-quality store-bought roti or naan, or steamed rice.

Use this vegetarian curry as a base for other vegetables. I love to add leafy greens, such as kale and spinach, or zucchini and broccoli. Make it your own and take the opportunity to use up any veggies in the crisper so they don't go to waste.

PANTRY STAPLES
Coconut milk
Coconut oil
Crispy fried shallots
Cumin seeds
Ground turmeric
Onion
Salt
Yellow split peas

SHOPPING LIST
Cauliflower
Fresh mint
Fresh small green
   chilli

POTATO TORTILLA

The simplest of foods are often the tastiest, like this Spanish omelette – or tortilla – made with eggs, potato and onion. The potato really is the hero of the dish and the egg acts as a binding agent. I use a smaller frying pan when I assemble the tortilla, as I like mine to be thick. Serve it with crusty bread and a juicy tomato salad and you'll almost feel like you're dining in a tapas bar in San Sebastian.

SERVES: 4   PREP: 15 MINUTES   COOK: 30 MINUTES

3 tomatoes
salt flakes and freshly ground
    black pepper
2 teaspoons red wine vinegar
    or sherry vinegar
125 ml (½ cup) olive oil
3 desiree potatoes (about 700 g),
    peeled and cut into 3 cm dice
1 onion, diced
6 eggs
3 tablespoons cream
crusty bread, to serve

Cut the tomatoes into bite-sized chunks and place on a serving plate. Season with salt and pepper, toss, then drizzle over the vinegar and 1 ½ tablespoons of oil. Leave at room temperature while you make the tortilla.

Rinse the potato and pat dry with a clean tea towel to remove a lot of the moisture.

Heat the remaining oil in a large frying pan over medium–high heat. Add the potato, toss to coat in the oil and cook for 5 minutes. Add the onion and fry, stirring regularly, for 15–20 minutes until soft and lightly coloured. Reduce the heat to medium if the potato and onion colour too quickly. Season with salt, then drain well, reserving the oil.

Whisk the eggs and cream with a pinch of salt in a large bowl. Add the potato mixture and stir to combine.

Heat another frying pan that is slightly smaller (about 24 cm in diameter) over medium heat – this will ensure the tortilla is not too thin, but if you like you can just use the same pan. Add 1 tablespoon of the reserved oil and swirl to coat the base and side of the pan. Pour in the egg and potato mixture and spread evenly. Poke the bottom of the pan with a wooden spoon to allow some of the egg mixture to seep through and set. Cook for 1–2 minutes, then shake and gently swirl the pan to detach the tortilla. Place a large plate over the pan and flip so the tortilla is on the plate, then carefully slide it back into the pan. Cook for a further 1 minute to seal the other side. I like my tortilla to be slightly runny in the centre, but if you prefer your eggs to be set, leave it in the pan for a little longer on each side. Flip onto a plate and serve hot with the tomatoes and crusty bread.

PANTRY STAPLES   **SHOPPING LIST**

Cream   Tomatoes
Crusty bread
Eggs
Olive oil
Onion
Potatoes
Red wine vinegar or
    sherry vinegar
Salt and pepper

For best results, cook the potatoes in a large frying pan so they become crispy and golden all over, then switch to a smaller frying pan to end up with a nice thick tortilla.

MUSHROOM RISOTTO

When it comes to risotto, it's not just about eating the finished dish, it's also about the process of making it; in fact, it's a really nice entertaining dish because guests can gather in the kitchen with the cook – and a glass of wine, of course – and watch the magical process unfold. This recipe is for my buddies Jess and Sven, who are mushroom risotto aficionados.

SERVES: 6, OR 4 VERY HUNGRY PEOPLE   PREP: 10 MINUTES   COOK: 35 MINUTES

1.3 litres chicken or vegetable stock
15 g dried porcini mushrooms
3 tablespoons olive oil
300 g mixed mushrooms
  (such as button, Swiss brown
  or oyster), cut or torn in half
50 g unsalted butter
salt flakes
1 small handful of flat-leaf parsley
  leaves, finely chopped
1 onion, finely diced
1 garlic clove, finely chopped
400 g arborio rice (see Note)
200 ml white wine (such as
  chardonnay or sauvignon blanc)
30 g parmesan, finely grated,
  plus extra to serve
freshly ground black pepper

Place the stock and porcini in a saucepan over low heat and bring to a gentle simmer.

Meanwhile, heat 2 tablespoons of oil in a large sauté pan over high heat, add the mixed mushrooms and toss to coat in the oil. Cook for 2–3 minutes, then add half the butter, a good pinch of salt and the parsley. Toss again and cook for a further 30 seconds. Transfer to a plate, cover and keep warm.

Wipe out the pan and place over medium–low heat. Add the remaining oil and stir in the onion, garlic and a pinch of salt and cook gently for 2–3 minutes until the onion is soft and translucent. Add the rice and stir to coat in the onion mixture. Continue to stir for 2 minutes until the rice loses its raw appearance and becomes shiny. Pour in the wine and bring to a simmer, stirring until the wine is completely absorbed.

Increase the heat to medium and start adding the stock to the pan. Add two ladlefuls of hot stock, including some rehydrated porcini in each ladleful, and stir two or three times. The rice will begin to release its starch and the mixture will start to look creamy. As the rice absorbs the liquid, keep adding more stock, two ladlefuls at a time, and tossing the pan until a couple of ladlefuls of stock remain. This process will take 15–17 minutes. The rice will be tender with a slightly chalky centre (al dente).

Now add the last of the stock to the pan. Turn off the heat and add the remaining butter, the parmesan and half of the cooked mushrooms and any juices that have collected on the plate. Cover and let rest for a minute. Taste for seasoning.

To serve, spoon the risotto onto serving plates. Tap the base of each plate so it spreads out evenly. Scatter over the remaining mushrooms, some extra parmesan and a good grind of pepper.

* Although standard supermarket arborio rice is perfectly fine to use, if you can get your hands on other varieties, such as carnaroli or vialone nano, it's well worth it as the risotto will be creamier and more refined. Delis and specialty stores stock these varieties.

PANTRY STAPLES
Arborio rice
Butter
Chicken or
  vegetable stock
Dried porcini
  mushrooms
Garlic
Olive oil
Onion
Parmesan
Salt and pepper
White wine

SHOPPING LIST
Fresh flat-leaf
  parsley
Mixed mushrooms

This very 'surf and turf' dish is a delightful combination of flavours made famous by the Portuguese and Spanish, who often cook pork with shellfish. I know a lot of people order mussels at a restaurant but won't cook them at home because they think they're too fiddly. Quite the opposite is true – they're easy to prepare and cook, affordable and readily available at fishmongers and most supermarkets (where they've been debearded and scrubbed, so are pot-ready). This recipe is a stand-out because the paprika- and garlic-laced chorizo works in harmony with the sweet, briny mussels.

SERVES: 2   PREP: 10 MINUTES   COOK: 20 MINUTES

1 onion, quartered

2 garlic cloves, peeled

100 g jarred roasted red capsicum, drained

1 chorizo sausage, casing removed and meat broken into chunks

2 tablespoons olive oil

2 tablespoons tomato paste

250 ml (1 cup) white wine (such as chardonnay or sauvignon blanc)

2 dried or fresh bay leaves

1 kg debearded and scrubbed black mussels, broken ones discarded

150 ml cream

salt flakes and freshly ground black pepper

crusty bread, to serve

Combine the onion, garlic and capsicum in a food processor. Blitz until finely chopped, then add the chorizo and pulse three or four times to combine.

Heat the oil in a large sauté pan over medium heat and add the chorizo mixture. Cook, stirring regularly, for 8–10 minutes until softened and lightly coloured. Add the tomato paste and cook for a further minute. Increase the heat to high, add the wine and bay leaves and bring to the boil. Cook until reduced by one-third, then add the mussels. Coat the mussels in the sauce, then put on the lid. Cook for 4–5 minutes, carefully shaking the pan halfway through so the mussels cook evenly. Using a slotted spoon, remove the mussels and place on a platter.

Add the cream to the pan and simmer for about 1–2 minutes to thicken. Taste and check the seasoning – the mussels and chorizo should be salty enough; if not, add a small pinch of salt and pepper. Pour the sauce over the mussels and serve in the middle of the table with lots of crusty bread.

PANTRY STAPLES

Bay leaves
Chorizo sausage
Cream
Crusty bread
Garlic
Jarred roasted red capsicum
Olive oil
Onion
Salt and pepper
Tomato paste
White wine

SHOPPING LIST

Mussels

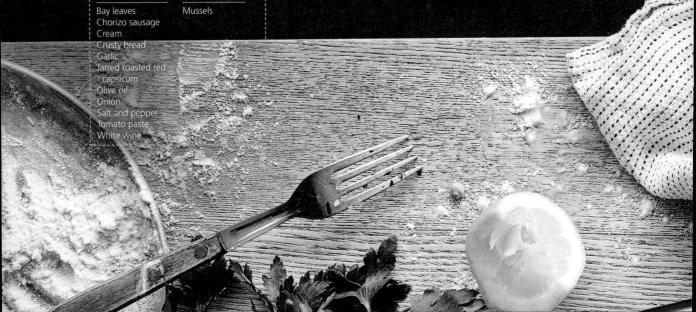

FLATHEAD WITH CAPER BUTTER

Mama Françoise would cook this simple French-style dish for us kids regularly, usually on a Friday night. Fuss-free and done in 15 minutes, it elevates the fish without overpowering it with too many flavours. I love to use flathead fillets as they're moist and flake easily; you could also try other white-fleshed fish, such as king george whiting, blue grenadier or snapper. This is lovely served with steamed baby potatoes and wilted spinach or any other vegetables you like.

SERVES: 4   PREP: 5 MINUTES   COOK: 10 MINUTES

plain flour, for dusting
salt flakes and freshly ground
   black pepper
4 x 120 g flathead fillets,
   pin-boned and skin removed
1 tablespoon olive oil
60 g butter
40 g baby capers in brine, drained
1 lemon
3 flat-leaf parsley sprigs,
   finely chopped

Season the flour with salt and pepper. Dust each fish fillet with the seasoned flour and shake off the excess.

Heat the oil in a large frying pan over medium–high heat and add the fish. Cook for 1–2 minutes, then flip the fish over and reduce the heat to medium. Add the butter and capers and cook, basting the fish in the butter, for about 1 minute until the butter starts to foam. Cook for a further 30–60 seconds, then transfer to a plate and keep warm.

Zest and juice half the lemon into the caper butter and add the parsley. Swirl the pan to combine and pour over the fish. Serve the fish with the remaining lemon, cut into chunks.

PANTRY STAPLES
Butter
Capers
Lemon
Olive oil
Plain flour
Salt and pepper

SHOPPING LIST
Flathead fillets
Fresh flat-leaf
   parsley

SALMON CAKES WITH TANGY TARTARE

This dish is perfect to make when you have leftover mash. I use two varieties of salmon for a lovely taste and texture, and also because they both have a long shelf life – meaning you are more likely to have them on hand when you want to whip up some fish cakes. Hot-smoked salmon is now available in most supermarkets; you'll find it in the chilled section near the smoked salmon.

SERVES: 4 PREP: 20 MINUTES, PLUS 15 MINUTES CHILLING
COOK: 35 MINUTES SUITABLE TO FREEZE

3 sebago potatoes (about 700 g), peeled and quartered
1 onion, finely chopped
4 dill fronds, chopped, plus extra to serve
4 flat-leaf parsley sprigs, leaves picked and chopped
3 tablespoons dijon mustard
100 g canned pink salmon, drained
300 g hot-smoked salmon, flaked
1 lemon, zested then cut into wedges
salt flakes and freshly ground black pepper
3 tablespoons whole-egg mayonnaise
3 tablespoons Greek yoghurt
1 tablespoon baby capers in brine, drained and chopped
1 gherkin, finely chopped
75 g (½ cup) plain flour
2 eggs
80 g (1 cup) fresh breadcrumbs
olive oil, for shallow-frying

Place the potato in a saucepan of cold salted water and bring to the boil. Cook for 20–25 minutes until tender. Drain in a colander and allow the steam to dissipate. While still hot, mash with a masher until smooth. Add half the onion and herbs and 2 tablespoons of mustard.

Place the remaining onion, herbs and mustard in a small bowl and set aside for the tartare sauce.

Add the canned and smoked salmon and lemon zest to the potato mixture and fold through with a fork, ensuring that the smoked salmon retains some flakiness. Season to taste. Divide the mixture into four, roll into balls and place on a lined tray. Cover and chill in the fridge for 10–15 minutes (or you can do this a day or two ahead).

To finish the tartare, add the mayonnaise, yoghurt, capers and gherkin to the onion and herb mixture. Mix well, then season with salt and pepper.

Place the flour in a shallow bowl. In another shallow bowl, lightly whisk the eggs with a pinch of salt. Place the breadcrumbs in a third bowl. Lightly flour each fish cake, dip in the egg wash and drain slightly, then coat in the breadcrumbs.

Heat the oil in a large frying pan over medium heat, add the fish cakes and cook for 2–3 minutes on each side until golden and crisp. Drain on paper towel and serve with the lemon wedges, tartare sauce and a final sprinkle of dill.

* You can use 2 cups of leftover mashed potato in the salmon cakes instead of the potato. Simply reheat until warm before adding the other ingredients.

Use dried breadcrumbs instead of fresh, if preferred.

PANTRY STAPLES	SHOPPING LIST
Canned salmon	Fresh dill
Capers	Fresh flat-leaf
Dijon mustard	parsley
Eggs	Hot-smoked
Fresh breadcrumbs	salmon
Gherkin	
Greek yoghurt	
Lemon	
Mayonnaise	
Olive oil	
Onion	
Plain flour	
Potatoes	
Salt and pepper	

SIMPLE SEAFOOD AND WHITE BEAN STEW

This brilliant one-pan wonder celebrates seafood and is hearty, yet elegant at the same time. The seafood I use for this dish is interchangeable. Depending on what I can get from the fishmonger, I like to change it up with the inclusion of mussels and scallops. Also, you can use any firm white-fleshed fish. Serve with crusty bread on the side and you've got a knock-out meal in no time.

SERVES: 4 **PREP:** 20 MINUTES **COOK:** 25 MINUTES

300 g small squid with tentacles, cleaned
3 tablespoons olive oil
2 garlic cloves, finely chopped
2 long red chillies, finely chopped (or 1 tablespoon sambal oelek)
2 anchovy fillets, finely chopped
125 g (½ cup) tomato passata
300 ml fish or chicken stock
1 x 400 g can white beans (such as cannellini), drained and rinsed
2 kale leaves, finely shredded, or 1 large handful of baby spinach leaves
salt flakes and freshly ground black pepper
4 x 150 g salmon fillets, pin-boned and skin removed, cut into 3 cm cubes
8 raw medium prawns, shelled and deveined with tails intact
grated zest and juice of ½ lemon
1 small handful of dill fronds and/or flat-leaf parsley leaves, finely chopped
Greek yoghurt or sour cream, to serve

Cut the squid tubes into thin rings, then chop each tentacle into four pieces.

Heat 1 tablespoon of oil in a sauté pan over high heat and flash-fry the squid for 30–60 seconds (any longer and it will become tough in the final dish). Remove from the pan and set aside.

Reduce the heat to medium, add the remaining oil and the garlic, chilli and anchovies to the pan and cook for about 1 minute until the garlic becomes light golden. Pour in the passata, bring to the boil and simmer for 3–4 minutes until thick and rich. Add the stock and return to the boil, then add the white beans and cook for 8–10 minutes. Mash some of the beans with a fork to thicken the sauce and add the kale or spinach, season with salt and pepper and cook for a further minute.

Add the salmon to the pan and cook for 1 minute. Next, add the prawns and cook for a minute before returning the squid and any juices in the bowl to the pan. Gently fold through, ensuring the salmon doesn't break up too much. Take off the heat and add the lemon zest and juice and herbs. Serve with a dollop of yoghurt or sour cream.

* If you want to speed things up, you can use 1 kg of seafood marinara mix instead (buy from your fishmonger or supermarket). Simply fry the marinara mix in two batches at the beginning of the method, then remove from the pan and continue cooking the vegetable and bean base. Return to the pan in the last step.

PANTRY STAPLES
Anchovies
Canned white beans
Fish stock or chicken stock
Garlic
Greek yoghurt or sour cream
Lemon
Olive oil
Salt and pepper
Tomato passata

SHOPPING LIST
Fresh dill and/or flat-leaf parsley
Fresh long red chillies
Kale or baby spinach
Raw prawns
Salmon fillets
Squid

SWEET AND SPICY BRAISED CHICKEN WINGS

I learned how to make this dish in a cooking class in Shanghai. I loved the notion of allowing the chicken to braise uncovered until most of the liquid had evaporated, leaving a lovely sticky glaze and tender, finger-licking wings. This is just brilliant as is, or even better with steamed jasmine or long-grain rice!

SERVES: 4   PREP: 10 MINUTES   COOK: 50 MINUTES

1–2 tablespoons sambal oelek (depending on how spicy you like it)
1 tablespoon kecap manis
1 tablespoon sugar
1 tablespoon vegetable oil
12 chicken wings (about 1.5 kg), separated at the joints and wing tips discarded
1 onion, sliced
2 star anise
375 ml (1½ cups) chicken stock
200 g green beans, topped and tailed, cut into 3 cm lengths

Combine the sambal oelek, kecap manis and sugar in a bowl.

Heat the oil in a wok or sauté pan over high heat. Add the wings, in batches, and cook for 1–2 minutes on each side until golden brown. Remove from the pan and set aside. Add the onion to the pan and fry for about 5 minutes until softened and golden in colour.

Return the chicken wings to the pan, add the sauce and star anise and toss to completely coat the chicken. Add the stock so the wings are just submerged (you can top up with a little water if needed). Reduce the heat to medium and simmer, turning the wings every 5 minutes, for 25–30 minutes until the chicken is almost falling off the bone and the sauce has thickened and reduced.

Add the beans to the pan and cook for 4–5 minutes until the sauce becomes a sticky, glossy glaze. Serve as is or with rice.

PANTRY STAPLES

Chicken stock
Kecap manis
Onion
Rice
Sambal oelek
Star anise
Sugar
Vegetable oil

SHOPPING LIST

Chicken wings
Green beans

KOREAN BACON AND EGG FRIED RICE

This is by no means a traditional Korean recipe, but it's fun to make and tastes sensational. It's one of those recipes to whip up when you don't have much time and want something bold and punchy in flavour. I add bacon, eggs, tofu and butter because I always have these staples in the fridge. I also always have kimchi on hand – it's great in this dish and as a side to lots of other dishes. Kimchi is readily available in delis and supermarkets.

SERVES: 4   PREP: 10 MINUTES   COOK: 10 MINUTES

6 streaky bacon rashers,
    roughly chopped
3 cm piece of ginger, grated
550 g (3 cups) cooked, day-old
    white rice (or use the packaged
    pre-cooked rice available from
    some supermarkets)
20 g unsalted butter
120 g (¾ cup) kimchi, finely
    chopped, plus extra to serve
2 tablespoons soy sauce
2 tablespoons honey
2 eggs, whisked
150 g silken tofu, cut into 4 pieces
4 spring onions, finely sliced
    on an angle

Put the bacon in a wok or large saucepan, then place over medium heat and cook for 2 minutes on each side until the fat renders and the bacon is crisp. Increase the heat to medium–high, add the ginger and fry for 30 seconds, then add the rice and butter. Toss the pan so the rice is coated in the ginger and bacon, then add the kimchi and any juices that have gathered on the chopping board. Toss again and allow the rice to toast in the pan for 1–2 minutes until crispy grains form on the base of the pan.

Combine the soy and honey in a bowl and add to the fried rice.

Using a wooden spoon, move the fried rice to one side of the pan, add the egg and stir to form ribbons of scrambled egg. While some parts of the egg are still runny, toss through the rice. Add the tofu and toss again. The tofu will break up, which is fine. Scatter on the spring onion and serve with some extra kimchi.

 Just like any other fried rice, to avoid a gluggy result and completely coat the grains in all the flavours, using day-old rice is essential.

Make this vegetarian by removing the bacon. If you like, you can substitute with mushrooms.

PANTRY STAPLES
Bacon
Butter
Eggs
Fresh ginger
Honey
Kimchi
Leftover cooked
    rice
Silken tofu
Soy sauce

SHOPPING LIST
Spring onions

GOT EGGS? GOT DINNER!

1. Bring homemade or store-bought hummus to room temperature, then spread over a shallow platter. Wilt handfuls of baby spinach leaves in a hot frying pan and scatter over the hummus. Fry eggs in olive oil in the same pan. Season with salt. Arrange on the spinach and sprinkle over some dukkah.

2. For a quick and interactive dinner, place a big bowl of baby cos lettuce leaves in the middle of the table. Add soft-boiled eggs, kimchi, sliced cucumber, freshly cooked rice, kecap manis and toasted sesame seeds. Now everyone can dig in and make their own Korean-style lettuce cups.

3. For eggs en cocotte, fry handfuls of diced mixed mushrooms in olive oil for a few minutes. Add garlic, flat-leaf parsley, salt and pepper and cook until fragrant. Portion into greased ovenproof ramekins. Make an indent in the middle of each and crack in an egg. Season, then add a pinch of nutmeg and a few tablespoons of cream. Place in a baking dish and pour in enough water to come halfway up the sides of the ramekins. Bake at 180°C for 10 minutes.

4. For super-tasty muffin omelettes, whisk 10 eggs with 3 tablespoons of cream. Add some baby spinach leaves, a large handful of grated cheddar, some chopped tomato and 4 chopped and fried bacon rashers. Pour into a standard 80 ml (⅓ cup) 12-hole muffin tin, then bake at 180°C for 15–20 minutes.

5. For a simple frittata, separate 4 eggs. Whisk the egg whites with a pinch of salt to form stiff peaks. In another bowl, whisk 3 tablespoons of fresh, full-fat ricotta until smooth. Mix in a small handful of grated parmesan, the egg yolks and a pinch of nutmeg and salt. Fold a third of the whites into the yolk mixture, then fold this into the remaining egg whites. Heat some olive oil in an ovenproof frying pan. Add the egg mixture and spread out. Bake at 180°C for 10 minutes.

6. For big-batch creamy scrambled eggs, crack 12 eggs into a non-stick saucepan and add 30 g of butter. Place over low heat. Using a silicone spatula, stir constantly for 5–6 minutes until custard-like. Pour in some cream, cook and stir until fluffy and glossy.

7. For soy-cured egg yolks, combine 250 ml (1 cup) of soy sauce and 2 tablespoons of caster sugar in a container. Mix to dissolve the sugar. Carefully submerge 6 egg yolks (be careful not to break them) in the soy mixture. Seal the container and cure for 6 hours in the fridge. Serve grated with fried rice or add to rice bowls with spicy fried beef mince or eggplant.

8. Fry some onion, dried oregano, garlic, red capsicum, eggplant and zucchini in olive oil. Add a 400 g can of whole peeled tomatoes. Cover and cook for 25 minutes until the vegetables are soft. Make six indents in the vegetable stew. Crack an egg into each cavity. Cover and cook for 8–10 minutes. Season and serve with crusty bread.

PORK SCHNITZEL WITH ARTICHOKES

Globe artichokes are one of my favourite vegetables. You can get them fresh at the beginning of spring, but for the rest of the year you can rely on the jarred alternative marinated in either oil or brine. The jarred variety is great to have in the pantry to jazz up a good old pork schnitzel (among other things). Artichokes have a sweet and nutty taste and they go particularly well with pork, but you can absolutely change the schnitzel to chicken or veal if you like.

SERVES: 4   PREP: 15 MINUTES   COOK: 20 MINUTES   SUITABLE TO FREEZE

1 x 500 g pork loin or scotch fillet (pork neck), trimmed of fat and cut into 4 even portions
75 g (½ cup) plain flour
2 eggs
salt flakes
200 g (2 cups) fine dry breadcrumbs
1 handful of freshly grated parmesan or pecorino
80 ml (⅓ cup) olive oil, plus 1 tablespoon extra
200 g marinated artichoke hearts, drained
1 small handful of chives, finely snipped
freshly ground black pepper
1 lemon, cut into wedges

Cover each piece of pork with baking paper and pound with a meat mallet or rolling pin to tenderise, flatten and spread into a thin steak.

Place the flour in a shallow bowl. In another shallow bowl, lightly beat the eggs with a pinch of salt. Combine the breadcrumbs and cheese in a third bowl.

Dust each piece of pork in the flour and shake off the excess, then dip in the egg wash and coat in the breadcrumb mixture, pressing on the crumbs.

Heat the oil in a large heavy-based frying pan over medium–high heat, add the crumbed pork, in two batches, and cook for 3–4 minutes on each side until golden brown. Remove, place in a single layer on a wire rack on a tray, and keep warm.

Combine the artichokes, chives, a pinch of salt and pepper, a squeeze of lemon juice and the extra olive oil in a bowl and mix well.

To serve, top each schnitzel with a spoonful of artichoke salad and serve with lemon wedges.

 Draining the schnitzels on a wire rack ensures they stay crisp on both sides.

To freeze, place each crumbed schnitzel between pieces of baking paper, then, in batches of two, cover with plastic wrap and freeze for up to 2 months. To cook, shallow-fry in oil directly from the freezer. No need to thaw.

The schnitzels are also great with a dollop of garlicky mayonnaise or mustard on the side.

PANTRY STAPLES
Dry breadcrumbs
Eggs
Lemon
Marinated artichoke hearts
Olive oil
Parmesan or pecorino
Plain flour
Salt and pepper

SHOPPING LIST
Fresh chives
Pork loin or scotch fillet

CRISPY BACON BANH MI

To use up extra bacon, I whipped up this famous street-food as a simple serving suggestion on my show Everyday Gourmet, *not imagining it would be such a big hit. So many people have asked for the recipe, and here it is. This irresistible French–Vietnamese sandwich is all about getting the ratio of ingredients right. Traditionally, banh mi is made with crispy pork. By all means roast some pork belly as a substitute for the bacon.*

SERVES: 4   PREP: 30 MINUTES   COOK: 10 MINUTES

8 streaky bacon rashers
4 crusty long bread rolls
125 g (½ cup) whole-egg mayonnaise
125 g chicken liver pâté (or any pâté of your choice)
1 Lebanese cucumber, deseeded and cut into long batons
4 spring onions, cut into thin strips
2 large handfuls of coriander leaves
1 long red chilli, finely sliced on an angle

PICKLED CARROT AND DAIKON
125 ml (½ cup) white vinegar
3 tablespoons sugar
1 teaspoon salt flakes
1 large carrot, julienned
¼ daikon, julienned

For the pickled carrot and daikon, bring the vinegar, sugar and salt to the boil in a small saucepan. Place the carrot in one bowl and the daikon in another and divide the pickling liquid between the two bowls. Cool and place in the fridge until ready to use. This can be done a few days ahead – store the veggies in airtight containers.

Arrange the bacon in a single layer in a large frying pan, place over medium heat and cook for about 2–3 minutes until the fat starts to render. Turn and cook for a few minutes more until crisp and golden. Drain on paper towel.

Cut the bread rolls in half horizontally, ensuring you don't cut all the way through. Spread the mayonnaise on one side and the pâté on the other side. Place two pieces of bacon on each roll, then add the drained pickled carrot and daikon, cucumber, spring onion, coriander leaves and a sprinkling of chilli.

PANTRY STAPLES
Bacon
Carrot
Mayonnaise
Salt
Sugar
White vinegar

SHOPPING LIST
Bread rolls
Chicken liver pâté
Daikon
Fresh coriander
Fresh long red chilli
Lebanese cucumber
Spring onions

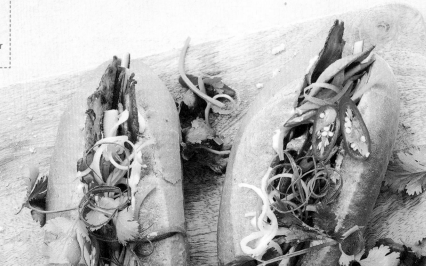

LENTILS AND SAUSAGES

*This is very much a French weeknight meal. I keep a variety of good-quality sausages
in the freezer for quick dinner ideas like this one. Lentils are a wonderful source of fibre
and are low in calories, which makes them a great substitute for potatoes, rice and pasta.
I like to serve this with a mixed leaf salad or some wilted spinach.*

SERVES: 4   PREP: 5 MINUTES   COOK: 30 MINUTES

200 g (1 cup) puy lentils (also called
   French green lentils)
1 celery stalk, cut into 3 cm pieces
1 carrot, cut into 3 cm pieces
1 onion, halved
1 dried bay leaf
1 tablespoon olive oil
6 thick pork sausages (about 500 g)
   (or any sausage of your choice)

TO SERVE
dijon mustard
sweet mustard pickles

Place the lentils, celery, carrot, onion and bay leaf in a saucepan,
cover with 750 ml (3 cups) of water and bring to the boil. Reduce
the heat to medium–low, cover and simmer for 25 minutes until
the lentils are tender.

While the lentils are cooking, heat a large heavy-based frying pan
over medium–high heat, drizzle in the oil and add the sausages.
Cook for 8–10 minutes, turning regularly, until the sausages are
cooked through.

Using a slotted spoon, transfer the lentils to a shallow dish (a little
of the cooking liquid is okay). Arrange the sausages on top and
serve with your favourite condiments. I like mustard and pickles.

PANTRY STAPLES
Bay leaf
Carrot
Dijon mustard
Olive oil
Onion
Pickles
Pork sausages
Puy lentils

SHOPPING LIST
Celery

* The best way to cook sausages is unpierced, which keeps them
lovely and juicy.

MINI DUMPLINGS IN CHILLI BROTH

Irresistible is the only way to describe these little bundles of joy: juicy pork and ginger encased in silky wonton wrappers and drenched in aromatic broth. The chilli broth has a real kick to it so feel free to reduce the sambal oelek to suit your palate – best to add half, taste and then add more if desired. Black vinegar has such depth of flavour – I highly recommend this as a pantry staple as it brings so much character to so many Asian dishes. You can find it at Asian grocers. Alternatively, you can use balsamic vinegar.

SERVES: 6   PREP: 1 HOUR   COOK: 10 MINUTES   SUITABLE TO FREEZE

1 ½ teaspoons cornflour
200 ml chicken stock
4 spring onions, white part
 finely chopped, pale green
 part julienned (see Note page 90)
350 g pork mince
3 cm piece of ginger, finely chopped
1 egg, whisked
100 ml soy sauce
60 square wonton wrappers
2 tablespoons sambal oelek
80 ml (⅓ cup) black vinegar
2 teaspoons sesame oil
3 tablespoons sugar

Place the cornflour and 2 tablespoons of stock in a small bowl and whisk to form a paste.

Place the white part of the spring onion in a bowl, add the pork mince, cornflour paste, ginger, egg and 1 tablespoon of soy sauce. Mix with a fork until a sticky paste forms.

Line a tray with baking paper.

Place a wonton wrapper on a clean work surface and add 1 teaspoon of the mince mixture to the centre. Brush the edges with a little water. Bring the opposite corners together and press to seal. Now lightly press around the filling to release any air bubbles and form a triangular parcel. Wrap the triangle around your thumb, bringing two of the three corners together. Brush one corner with a little water and press to stick together. It should look like a little hat or rough tortellini. Place on the prepared tray and cover with a damp cloth to ensure it does not dry out. Repeat with the remaining wrappers and mince mixture.

Meanwhile, combine the sambal oelek, black vinegar, sesame oil, sugar and remaining soy and stock in a small saucepan and warm through for about 2 minutes until the sugar dissolves.

Bring a large saucepan of water to a simmer. Add the dumplings, in two batches if necessary, and cook for 4–5 minutes until they rise to the surface. Remove with a slotted spoon and arrange in a shallow dish. It's okay if a little starchy water goes into the dish, this will simply add to the broth and keep the dumplings moist. Pour over the hot chilli broth and serve with the green part of the spring onion scattered over the top.

PANTRY STAPLES   **SHOPPING LIST**
Black vinegar   Spring onions
Chicken stock
Cornflour
Egg
Fresh ginger
Pork mince
Sambal oelek
Sesame oil
Soy sauce
Sugar
Wonton wrappers

✳ These dumplings freeze really well, so you may like to freeze half – they are great to have on standby for a quick dinner. Simply cover the uncooked dumplings with plastic wrap and freeze on the tray. Once completely frozen, transfer the wontons to a zip-lock bag. Cook directly from the freezer.

PORK SOUVLAKI

We often think of lamb as the hero meat in Greek food, particularly souvlaki wraps, but in Greece when you go to a yeeros or souvlaki bar, the options are usually pork or chicken. Pork is a great option because as it cooks the fat melts, keeping the meat super moist. This recipe is perfect for entertaining large groups of people and can easily be multiplied. The meat can be marinated and threaded onto skewers the night before and the tzatziki can be prepared then, too. Simple and delicious.

SERVES: 4–6   PREP: 25 MINUTES, PLUS AT LEAST 15 MINUTES MARINATING
COOK: 15 MINUTES

2 teaspoons dried oregano,
  plus extra to serve
1 teaspoon coriander seeds,
  plus extra crushed seeds to serve
grated zest and juice of ½ lemon
1½ garlic cloves, finely chopped
2 tablespoons extra-virgin olive oil
salt flakes and freshly ground
  black pepper
1 x 1.2 kg pork scotch fillet
  (pork neck) or pork belly,
  rind and sinew removed,
  cut into 3 cm cubes
6 pita breads
2 tomatoes, halved and sliced
½ onion, finely sliced

TZATZIKI
2 Lebanese cucumbers, peeled,
  deseeded and coarsely grated
salt flakes
½ garlic clove, finely chopped
250 g (1 cup) Greek yoghurt
extra-virgin olive oil, for drizzling

PANTRY STAPLES
Coriander seeds
Dried oregano
Extra-virgin olive oil
Garlic
Greek yoghurt
Lemon
Pita bread
Salt and pepper

SHOPPING LIST
Lebanese
  cucumbers
Pork scotch fillet
  or belly
Tomatoes

If using wooden skewers, soak them in warm water for 10 minutes. This ensures the skewers won't splinter and burn while cooking. Metal skewers are fine to use, too.

Combine the oregano, coriander seeds, lemon zest and juice, garlic, oil and a generous pinch of salt and pepper in a large glass or ceramic container. Add the pork and massage the marinade into the meat. Thread six to eight pieces of meat onto each skewer, ensuring there are no gaps. Leave at room temperature to marinate for 15–20 minutes or, even better, cover and place in the fridge to marinate overnight.

For the tzatziki, place the cucumber in a sieve and add a good pinch of salt. Stand for 5 minutes, then squeeze out as much liquid as possible. Place in a bowl with the garlic, yoghurt, a pinch of salt and a drizzle of olive oil. Mix and refrigerate until ready to use.

Preheat the oven to 180°C.

Heat a large chargrill pan over medium–high heat or the barbecue to medium–hot. (If cooking inside, I highly recommend opening all the windows, as it is going to get smoky!) Add the skewers, in batches if necessary, and cook, turning and basting frequently, for 12–15 minutes until nicely charred.

Meanwhile, stack the pitas in piles of three, wrap in foil and warm in the oven for 10 minutes.

To serve, dollop a spoonful of tzatziki into the centre of a pita, add some tomato and onion slices, then slide the hot meat off the skewers and place on top. Sprinkle with a little extra oregano and crushed coriander and wrap up.

* For a richer, creamier tzatziki, line a sieve with a double layer of muslin or two clean Chux cloths and place over a large bowl. Spoon in 500 g (2 cups) of Greek yoghurt, then bring the sides of the cloth together and tie with a rubber band. Refrigerate for 2–3 hours. Discard the liquid that collects in the bowl (or save it for smoothies). The strained yoghurt is ready to use in your tzatziki.

SALTIMBOCCA

Saltimbocca is Italian and translates as 'jump in the mouth'. It's the perfect description because the combination of mild veal, salty prosciutto and the strong musty perfume of sage is a sensational flavour bomb. I've also made this recipe with thin slices of pork and chicken, so change it up depending on what you like. Serve simply with green beans or with the Spinach Gratin on page 26.

SERVES: 4   PREP: 15 MINUTES   COOK: 10 MINUTES

4 veal escalopes (each about 150 g)
8 thin slices of prosciutto
8 sage leaves
1 tablespoon olive oil
plain flour, for dusting
20 g butter
100 ml white wine
125 ml (½ cup) chicken stock

Place the veal escalopes between two pieces of baking paper. Using the flat side of a meat mallet or a rolling pin, pound to tenderise and flatten, then cut into two even-sized pieces. Pound each piece until very flat. You will have eight 75 g pieces. Cover one side of each veal steak with the prosciutto, top with two sage leaves and fasten with a toothpick.

Heat the oil in a large frying pan over medium–high heat. Lightly dust both sides of the veal with the flour, then add to the pan, prosciutto-side up. Cook for 1 minute, then turn over and add the butter to the pan. Cook the veal for a further minute, then remove from the pan and place on a plate, covering to keep warm.

Deglaze the pan with the white wine and bring to the boil. Add the stock and cook until reduced by one-third. Pour the juices over the veal and serve.

PANTRY STAPLES
Butter
Chicken stock
Olive oil
Plain flour
White wine

SHOPPING LIST
Fresh sage
Prosciutto
Veal escalopes

SIZZLING BEEF WITH RICE NOODLES

This stir-fry brings together two ingredients I love so much: fresh rice noodles and peppery steak. It's a spin on the Vietnamese dish shaking beef (bo luc lac), but instead of serving the meat by itself, I take things up a notch and toss it with silky noodles. The beautiful thing about a stir-fry is that you can add lots of different vegetables. I've kept mine very basic, so you can be the master chef and add your own twist.

SERVES: 4   **PREP:** 15 MINUTES, PLUS 10 MINUTES MARINATING   **COOK:** 5 MINUTES

2 tablespoons oyster sauce
1 tablespoon caster sugar
1 teaspoon sesame oil
500 g rump steak, finely sliced
2 tablespoons vegetable oil
1 onion, quartered and
   layers separated
2 cm piece of ginger, finely chopped
2 heads of bok choy,
   quartered lengthways
1 teaspoon black peppercorns,
   crushed
450 g fresh rice noodles
   (or 200 g dried pad Thai
   noodles), prepared as per
   packet instructions
1 tablespoon soy sauce
juice of ½ lemon

Combine the oyster sauce, sugar and sesame oil in a large glass or ceramic bowl. Add the steak and toss to coat, then marinate for 5–10 minutes at room temperature.

Heat half the oil in a wok or large frying pan over high heat, add the steak, in batches, and cook for 20–30 seconds to seal and scorch slightly. Transfer to a plate and set aside.

Heat the remaining oil in the wok or pan, add the onion, ginger and bok choy and stir-fry for 1 minute until the onion is lightly caramelised. Now add the pepper and toss a few times before returning the meat, and any juices on the plate, to the pan. Add the noodles, soy sauce and lemon juice and toss to warm the noodles and coat the meat in the sauce. Serve immediately.

PANTRY STAPLES

Black peppercorns
Caster sugar
Fresh ginger
Lemon
Onion
Oyster sauce
Sesame oil
Soy sauce
Vegetable oil

SHOPPING LIST

Bok choy
Fresh rice noodles
   or dried pad Thai
   noodles
Rump steak

AFGHAN DUMPLINGS

Many cultures have their own style of dumpling; in this case it's an Afghan variety called 'mantu'. Afghanistan borders China, Iran and Pakistan, and you can see their culinary influence in these dumplings with the addition of spices, a garlicky yoghurt sauce, dried mint and wonton wrappers. Traditionally, the meat is cooked prior to filling the wrapper, but I like to skip that part to speed up the process. I find the end result is juicier, too.

SERVES: 6   **PREP:** 40 MINUTES   **COOK:** 30 MINUTES   **SUITABLE TO FREEZE**

2 tablespoons olive oil
2 onions, finely chopped
salt flakes
1 x 400 g can whole peeled
   tomatoes, crushed
1 x 400 g can lentils, drained
   and rinsed
freshly ground black pepper
250 g fatty beef mince
½ teaspoon ground coriander
½ teaspoon ground cumin
½ teaspoon dried mint,
   plus extra to serve
30 round wonton wrappers
250 g (1 cup) Greek yoghurt
1 garlic clove, finely chopped
grated zest and juice of ½ lemon

Heat the oil in a sauté pan over medium heat and add the onion and a pinch of salt. Fry for 3–4 minutes until softened and lightly coloured. Remove half the onion and place in a large bowl to cool.

Tip the tomatoes into the pan, then half-fill the can with water, pour that in and bring to the boil. Add the lentils, season with salt and pepper and cook for 12–15 minutes until the sauce is thick and rich. Cover with a lid to keep warm and set aside.

Meanwhile, combine the mince, reserved onion, spices, dried mint and a pinch of salt in a bowl and mix with a fork.

Working in batches of ten, place the wonton wrappers on a clean work surface and add 1 heaped teaspoon of mince mixture to the centre of each. Brush the edges with a little water, then fold and press to seal. Now lightly press around the meat filling to release any air bubbles and form a half-moon shape. Place on a tray and cover with a damp cloth to ensure they do not dry out. Repeat with the remaining wrappers and mince mixture.

Combine the yoghurt, garlic, lemon zest and juice and a pinch of salt in a bowl. Spread half on a large platter.

Bring a large saucepan of salted water to the boil and add the dumplings – you may need to do this in two batches so you don't overcrowd the pan. Cook for 3–4 minutes until they begin to float to the surface, then remove with a slotted spoon and drain well. Place on top of the yoghurt mixture.

Spoon the warm lentil sauce over the dumplings, drizzle on the remaining yoghurt mixture and sprinkle with extra dried mint.

✽ The dumplings can be made a day ahead and stored in an airtight container in the fridge until ready to cook. They freeze well, too.

PANTRY STAPLES   **SHOPPING LIST**

Beef mince
Canned lentils
Canned whole
  peeled tomatoes
Dried mint
Garlic
Greek yoghurt
Ground coriander
Ground cumin
Lemon
Olive oil
Onions
Salt and pepper
Wonton wrappers

STEAK FOR TWO

Cooking a steak for two is so very romantic. If you follow a few key rules, such as bringing the meat to room temperature, seasoning well and resting, then I can guarantee you'll become an expert at cooking steak in no time.

SERVES: 2   PREP: 5 MINUTES, PLUS 5 MINUTES RESTING   COOK: 10 MINUTES

650 g rib-eye steak, bone in,
    brought to room temperature
    for 1 hour (see Note)
1 teaspoon olive oil
salt flakes
20 g cold butter
4 thyme sprigs
2 fresh bay leaves (optional)
freshly ground black pepper
dijon mustard, to serve

Heat a large frying pan over medium–high heat. Pat the steak dry with paper towel, massage in the oil, then season generously with salt. Add the steak to the pan and cook for 2 minutes, then turn and cook for a further 2 minutes. Turn again and cook for 2 minutes, turn, add the butter, thyme and bay leaves and cook, basting the steak as the butter starts to foam, for 2 minutes for medium–rare. Season with pepper, then remove from the pan and place on a clean chopping board to rest for 4–5 minutes. (The steak retains its residual heat, so it won't get cold. Resting is important to ensure the meat stays super juicy. Don't skip this step.)

Slice the meat off the bone, cut into 2 cm thick slices and present on a plate beside the bone. Top with the thyme and bay leaves and serve with the pan juices and some mustard on the side.

 Bringing the steak to room temperature before cooking is crucial to ensure the meat cooks evenly. Simply remove the steak from the fridge 1 hour before cooking, place on a plate and cover with baking paper.

You can also serve this with my Super-crunchy Roast Potatoes on page 25. If including, start on the potatoes while the steak is coming to room temperature. And if you really want to impress you should also make Aunty Vero's Crusted Tomatoes on page 32 as a side.

PANTRY STAPLES
Butter
Dijon mustard
Olive oil
Salt and pepper

SHOPPING LIST
Fresh bay leaves
Fresh thyme
Rib-eye steak

LAMB CUTLETS WITH WARM ANCHOVY AND CAPER DRESSING

It may seem like an unlikely pairing, but anchovies work very nicely with lamb. In fact, they enhance the flavour of the lamb, giving it a kick of savouriness. This dish will not taste at all fishy, as once the anchovies are cooked they melt down to make a fragrant warm dressing. Fantastic with warm white bean puree, this is also delicious served with crispy roast potatoes (page 25).

SERVES: 4   PREP: 15 MINUTES   COOK: 10 MINUTES

80 ml (⅓ cup) extra-virgin olive oil
12 lamb cutlets, French trimmed
salt flakes and freshly ground
    black pepper
3 anchovy fillets
1 garlic clove, peeled
3 tablespoons baby capers in brine,
    drained, plus 1 tablespoon brine
2 large handfuls of rocket leaves
    (or any leafy green)

WHITE BEAN PUREE

1 x 400 g can white beans (such as
    cannellini), drained and rinsed
juice of ½ lemon
1 garlic clove, finely chopped
80 ml (⅓ cup) extra-virgin olive oil
pinch of salt flakes (optional)

To make the white bean puree, place the white beans, lemon juice and garlic in a food processor and blitz until a thick paste forms. With the motor running, slowly drizzle in the oil and process until combined. If the puree is too thick, mix in a little warm water. Taste and add salt if required. Transfer to a saucepan, place over low heat and cook, stirring occasionally, until warm. Cover with the lid and set aside.

Drizzle 1 tablespoon of oil over the lamb and massage all over, then season with salt and pepper.

Finely chop the anchovies and garlic together and, with the side of your knife, squash them to make a rough paste. Alternatively, pound together using a mortar and pestle.

Heat a large heavy-based frying pan over medium–high heat, add the lamb cutlets and cook for 2–3 minutes on each side until golden brown. You may need to do this in two batches. Transfer to a plate and set aside to rest for 5 minutes in a warm place.

Heat the remaining 3 tablespoons of olive oil in the frying pan over medium–high heat. Add the drained capers and cook for 1–2 minutes until very crisp. Remove with a slotted spoon and set aside.

Add the anchovy mixture to the hot oil and cook for 30 seconds, then remove from the heat and stir through the caper brine.

Place the cutlets on plates and add the peppery rocket leaves and a generous drizzle of warm anchovy dressing. Serve with the warm white bean puree on the side.

PANTRY STAPLES
Anchovy fillets
Capers
Extra-virgin olive oil
Garlic
Salt and pepper
White wine vinegar

SHOPPING LIST
Lamb cutlets
Rocket leaves

* The white bean puree can be made a few days in advance and kept in an airtight container in the fridge. Before placing the lid on top, cover the surface of the puree with plastic wrap to ensure a skin does not form. Gently warm through just before serving.

BATCH COOKING

TOMATO SOUP WITH CHEESE TOASTIES

When we were kids, most Sundays my family would drive to Moss Vale in country New South Wales to visit my gran. We loved it because the tradition was to have canned tomato soup and buttered square bread for lunch. This spin on tomato soup is easy to make and most of the ingredients can be found in your pantry and fridge. I use canned tomatoes and, to ensure they are not too acidic, balance the flavours with butter and cream. I serve my soup with cheese toasties, for the ultimate comfort food pairing.

SERVES: 4   PREP: 10 MINUTES   COOK: 35 MINUTES

25 g butter, plus extra
   for buttering bread
1 onion, chopped
2 garlic cloves, chopped
½ teaspoon chilli flakes (or to taste),
   plus extra to serve, if desired
½ teaspoon dried oregano, plus
   extra to serve, if desired
2 bay leaves
2 tablespoons tomato paste
3 x 400 g cans whole peeled
   tomatoes
salt flakes and freshly ground
   black pepper
1 teaspoon sugar
1 litre chicken or vegetable stock
150 ml cream
8 slices of white bread
1 tablespoon dijon mustard
125 g sharp cheddar, grated

Melt the butter in a large saucepan over medium heat and add the onion, garlic, chilli flakes, dried oregano and bay leaves. Cook, stirring regularly, for 4–5 minutes until the onion is softened but not coloured. Add the tomato paste and cook for a further 1 minute, then add the tomatoes and crush with a wooden spoon. Bring to the boil and season with salt and pepper and the sugar. Pour in the stock and bring to the boil. Reduce the heat to medium–low, cover and cook for 20–25 minutes. Remove from the heat and blend with a hand-held blender until smooth. Add the cream and blend to incorporate. Check the seasoning again and adjust if necessary.

Meanwhile, butter one side of each piece of bread. Spread a teaspoon of mustard on four unbuttered sides, sprinkle on the cheese and top with the remaining bread slices, buttered-side up. Heat a frying pan over medium–low heat, add the sandwiches, in batches, and cook for 3 minutes on each side, turning regularly. Alternatively, toast in a sandwich press. Cut the toasties in half.

Ladle the soup into bowls and serve with the cheese toasties and an extra sprinkle of chilli flakes and oregano, if you like.

PANTRY STAPLES   **SHOPPING LIST**

Bay leaves
Bread
Butter
Canned tomatoes
Cheddar
Chicken or
  vegetable stock
Chilli flakes
Cream
Dijon mustard
Dried oregano
Garlic
Onion
Salt and pepper
Sugar
Tomato paste

BROCCOLI CANNELLONI

Cannelloni is often filled with a meat sauce or spinach and ricotta, but I love to change it up by filling the tubes with creamy broccoli. This is a really tasty vegetarian dish the whole family will like. Don't be put off by the long list of ingredients; you'll already have many of these items in your fridge and pantry.

To get this on the table more quickly, you can prepare the broccoli filling and white sauce a day ahead.

SERVES: 4   PREP: 30 MINUTES   COOK: 1 HOUR

1 tablespoon olive oil, plus extra
   for greasing
2 heads of broccoli (about 700 g)
1 small handful of basil leaves
2 tablespoons pine nuts
300 g fresh, full-fat ricotta
1 garlic clove, peeled
grated zest of 1 lemon
½ teaspoon chilli flakes
700 g tomato passata
salt flakes and freshly ground
   black pepper
255 g cannelloni
1 buffalo mozzarella ball, torn

WHITE SAUCE
20 g butter
1 ½ tablespoons plain flour
300 ml milk
pinch of freshly grated nutmeg
30 g parmesan, finely grated

PANTRY STAPLES
Butter
Cannelloni
Chilli flakes
Garlic
Lemon
Milk
Nutmeg
Olive oil
Parmesan
Pine nuts
Plain flour
Ricotta
Salt and pepper
Tomato passata

SHOPPING LIST
Broccoli
Buffalo mozzarella
Fresh basil

Preheat the oven to 180°C. Grease a large baking dish (about 42 cm x 28 cm) with a little oil.

Cut the broccoli into florets, then peel the stems and cut into rough chunks.

Bring a saucepan of salted water to the boil, add the broccoli and cook for 8–10 minutes until tender. Drain and cool a little.

Place the basil, pine nuts, ricotta, garlic, lemon and chilli flakes in a food processor and blend until smooth. Add the broccoli and pulse four or five times to puree. Scoop into a piping bag or a zip-lock bag with one corner snipped off.

Pour the tomato passata into the prepared dish. Drizzle over 1 tablespoon of olive oil and season with salt and pepper.

For the white sauce, melt the butter in a saucepan over medium heat, add the flour and stir constantly for 2–3 minutes with a wooden spoon. Remove the pan from the heat and pour in a quarter of the milk, whisking vigorously to prevent lumps. Place back on the heat and stir in the rest of the milk. Whisk until the sauce comes to the boil and thickens. Remove from the heat, season with the nutmeg and salt and pepper and stir in half the parmesan until melted and combined.

Pipe the broccoli mixture into each cannelloni tube. Arrange the filled cannelloni side by side on the tomato passata. Pour on the white sauce and spread evenly over the top to ensure the cannelloni are covered. Scatter over the mozzarella and the remaining parmesan, cover with foil and bake for 20 minutes. Remove the foil and bake for a further 20–25 minutes until the top is golden brown.

CARROT AND TURMERIC SOUP

Apart from giving this soup an extra bright pop of colour, the bitter floral flavour of turmeric pairs beautifully with the sweetness of the carrot. If you can get your hands on fresh turmeric, one teaspoon, finely grated, will take your soup to the next level.

I always have this soup on standby in the freezer for a quick and very healthy lunch or light dinner.

SERVES: 4   PREP: 10 MINUTES   COOK: 35 MINUTES   SUITABLE TO FREEZE

1 tablespoon olive oil, plus extra
   for drizzling
1 onion, chopped
1 teaspoon ground turmeric
1 kg carrots, cut into 2 cm rounds
salt flakes
1.8 litres chicken or vegetable stock
   or water
1 small handful of flat-leaf
   parsley leaves
3 tablespoons shaved parmesan
freshly ground black pepper

Heat the oil in a large saucepan over medium–high heat. Add the onion and cook for 2–3 minutes to soften, then add the turmeric and stir to coat the onion.

Add the carrot to the pan and season with a small pinch of salt. Pour in the stock or water and bring to the boil. Reduce the heat to low and gently simmer for 25–30 minutes until the carrot is soft. Blend with a hand-held blender until silky smooth.

Serve with a sprinkle of parsley, parmesan and pepper and finish with a drizzle of olive oil.

* If you feel like getting a bit fancy, try frying the parsley leaves to garnish as we've done here.

PANTRY STAPLES

Carrots
Chicken or
   vegetable stock
Ground turmeric
Olive oil
Onion
Parmesan
Salt and pepper

SHOPPING LIST

Fresh flat-leaf
   parsley

ZUCCHINI SPANAKOPITA

I like to call this a 'spanakopita' as it's made the very same way as the classic spinach version; however, in Greece, zucchini baked in filo is called 'kolokythopita'. Either way, this savoury pie is to die for. The grated zucchini cooks down to become sweet and silky, and is then wrapped in flaky filo. It's a beautiful recipe to add to your repertoire, and is great served warm or cold, making it perfect for your next barbecue or picnic.

SERVES: 4   PREP: 20 MINUTES   COOK: 1 HOUR 5 MINUTES

100 g butter, melted
2 tablespoons olive oil
1 onion, finely chopped
600 g zucchini (about 3), coarsely grated
½ teaspoon dried oregano
salt flakes
500 g fresh, full-fat ricotta
200 g feta, crumbled
1 ½ tablespoons finely chopped dill fronds
3 eggs
freshly ground black pepper
12 sheets of filo pastry
3 tablespoons sesame seeds

Preheat the oven to 180°C. Grease a 25 cm round baking dish with a little melted butter.

Heat the oil in a sauté pan over medium heat, add the onion and cook for 3–4 minutes until softened. Stir in the zucchini, dried oregano and a pinch of salt. Cover and cook, stirring regularly, for 6–8 minutes until the zucchini is very soft and the liquid has evaporated. Cool to room temperature.

Place the ricotta, feta, dill and eggs in a large bowl and combine with a wooden spoon. Season with a small pinch of salt and pepper, then fold in the cooled zucchini mixture.

Cover the filo pastry with a damp tea towel (this stops it from drying out). Working with one sheet at a time, brush the filo with the remaining melted butter and place in the prepared dish. Repeat, allowing the next seven layers to come up the side and overlap (just like patchwork). Add the zucchini filling and spread all the way to the edge, then fold the overhanging filo over the filling. Brush the remaining five sheets of filo with melted butter and, one by one, layer over the top, tucking in any overhanging pastry to form a neat pie. Brush the top with the last of the melted butter and sprinkle on the sesame seeds. Bake for 45–50 minutes until golden brown. Cool for 20 minutes before removing or slicing in the dish. Serve warm or cold.

* Filo pastry can be bought at delis and most supermarkets. I always buy an extra packet and keep it in the freezer so I can whip up this pie at the drop of a hat. Ensure you allow it to thaw before you begin the recipe.

This filling is really versatile so if you have leftover roasted vegetables, such as sweet potato or pumpkin, simply mix them through with the cheese and eggs.

PANTRY STAPLES
Butter
Dried oregano
Eggs
Feta
Filo pastry
Olive oil
Onion
Ricotta
Salt and pepper
Sesame seeds

SHOPPING LIST
Fresh dill
Zucchini

TWICE-COOKED SOUFFLÉS

Ahhh, twice-cooked soufflés. I can hear your sigh of relief – no need to worry about deflating soufflés! I love this recipe as you can make your soufflés ahead of time – I bake mine in a muffin tin – then simply pour over the decadent sauce and bake again when you're ready to serve. These are great served with a crisp green salad for lunch (very French to do this) or a light dinner, or impress your guests and make them as an entrée at your next dinner party.

MAKES: 12   **PREP:** 20 MINUTES   **COOK:** 1 HOUR 15 MINUTES   **SUITABLE TO FREEZE**

80 g unsalted butter, plus extra
    for greasing
80 g plain flour, plus extra
    for dusting
500 ml (2 cups) full-cream milk
½ teaspoon freshly grated nutmeg
160 g Gruyère or cheddar cheese
salt flakes and freshly ground
    black pepper
5 eggs, separated
2 tablespoons dry sherry
500 ml (2 cups) cream
3 thyme sprigs, leaves picked
50 g parmesan, finely grated

Preheat the oven to 180°C. Grease a standard (80 ml) 12-hole muffin tin with butter and dust with a little flour, tapping out any excess.

Melt the butter in a saucepan over medium heat, add the flour and cook, stirring constantly, for 2 minutes until the roux is golden and combined. Gradually whisk in the milk and cook, whisking constantly, for 3 minutes until the sauce becomes thick and glossy with no lumps. Remove from the heat, add the nutmeg and half the Gruyère or cheddar and season with salt and pepper. Remove from the heat and allow to cool for 5 minutes, then mix in the egg yolks.

Place the egg whites and a pinch of salt in a bowl and whisk until stiff peaks form. Add one-third of the egg whites to the white sauce and fold in. Carefully fold in another third and, finally, gently fold in the last third.

Fill the prepared tin with the soufflé mixture and smooth out with the back of a spoon to ensure the holes are evenly filled. Wipe away any drips on the tin with paper towel. Bake for 20–25 minutes until the soufflés are puffed and golden. Do not open the oven door while they are cooking. Cool for 15 minutes – they will deflate – then carefully loosen and remove from the tin using a small palette knife or butter knife. (At this point, the soufflés can be placed in the fridge or frozen for use at a later date.) Place the soufflés in individual ovenproof dishes or side by side in one large baking dish.

Combine the sherry, cream and thyme in a saucepan and bring to the boil for 6–8 minutes to thicken. Pour evenly over the soufflés. Mix the remaining Gruyère or cheddar with the parmesan and sprinkle over the top. Return to the oven to bake for 25–30 minutes until golden and bubbling. Serve warm.

PANTRY STAPLES
Cream
Eggs
Full-cream milk
Nutmeg
Parmesan
Plain flour
Salt and pepper
Sherry
Unsalted butter

SHOPPING LIST
Fresh thyme
Gruyère or cheddar

CHICKEN AND MUSHROOM COTTAGE PIE

Cottage pie is usually made with beef or lamb, but I sometimes like to change up the meat component – in this instance, the filling is a quick chicken stew. The stew itself is worth making because that traditional pairing of cream and mushrooms is always so satisfying. Crowned with lashings of creamy mashed potato . . . well, what more can I say? A lot of people are going to love you for making this for them!

SERVES: 4–6   PREP: 15 MINUTES   COOK: 1 HOUR 30 MINUTES

2 tablespoons olive oil, plus extra
   for drizzling
800 g boneless, skinless chicken
   thighs, each cut into 4 pieces
salt flakes and freshly ground
   black pepper
1 leek, white and pale green part
   only, finely chopped
160 g speck or streaky bacon,
   cut into lardons
350 g button mushrooms, quartered
3 thyme sprigs, leaves picked
200 ml white wine (see Note)
1 tablespoon dijon mustard
pinch of cayenne pepper
250 ml (1 cup) chicken stock
150 g crème fraîche or sour cream
20 g parmesan, grated
1 tablespoon panko breadcrumbs

MASH

6 sebago or desiree potatoes (1 kg),
   peeled and quartered
salt flakes
50 g butter
125 ml (½ cup) hot milk
freshly ground black pepper

To make the mash, place the potato in a saucepan, cover with cold water and add a pinch of salt. Bring to the boil and cook for 20 minutes until the potato is soft. Drain in a colander and allow the steam to dissipate. Return the potato to the pan and mash, then add the butter. Keep mashing until the butter has melted into the potato, then pour in the hot milk. Whip the milk through with a wooden spoon until a smooth, thick mash forms. Check the seasoning and add a pinch of pepper. Cover with the lid and reserve for later.

Heat 1 tablespoon of oil in a large sauté pan over high heat. Add the chicken, season with salt and pepper and cook for 4–5 minutes until lightly coloured. Remove from the pan to a plate and set aside. Reduce the heat to medium. Add the remaining oil, the leek and speck or bacon to the pan and sauté for 3–4 minutes. Stir in the mushrooms and thyme and cook for a further 3–4 minutes until softened.

Preheat the oven to 200°C.

Return the chicken and any juices on the plate to the pan. Stir well and deglaze the pan with the wine. Bring to the boil, then mix in the mustard and add the cayenne pepper and stock. Reduce the heat to low and simmer for 10 minutes until reduced by one-third. Mix through the crème fraîche or sour cream and cook for 3–4 minutes until thick enough to coat the back of a spoon.

Pour the chicken stew into a 2 litre baking dish and spread out evenly. Dollop the mash over the top and, with the back of a spoon or a fork, spread to cover (make a swirly pattern if you like). Sprinkle over the cheese and breadcrumbs and drizzle with a little extra olive oil. Place the dish on a baking tray and transfer to the oven. Bake for 25–30 minutes until golden on top.

* I like to use chardonnay or sauvignon blanc in this recipe, but any white wine is fine.

PANTRY STAPLES

Butter
Cayenne pepper
Chicken stock
Dijon mustard
Leek
Milk
Olive oil
Panko breadcrumbs
Parmesan
Potatoes
Salt and pepper
White wine

SHOPPING LIST

Button mushrooms
Chicken thighs
Crème fraîche or
  sour cream
Fresh thyme
Speck or bacon

CAN-DO MEALS

1. Combine 425 g of drained canned tuna, a handful of grated parmesan and frozen peas and 2 cups of leftover risotto or cooked rice. Shape into walnut-sized balls. Insert a piece of torn mozzarella into each ball and roll again to enclose the mozzarella. Dust in plain flour, dunk in whisked egg, then coat in breadcrumbs. Shallow-fry in olive oil over medium–high heat until crispy and golden.

2. Pulse a 400 g can of drained and rinsed white beans, 1 finely chopped garlic clove, juice of ½ lemon, 80 ml (⅓ cup) of extra-virgin olive oil and a pinch of salt in a food processor three or four times to roughly puree. If too thick, add a little warm water. Warm up slightly just before serving with lamb or fish.

3. For a quick tray bake, combine 3 chopped tomatoes, a chopped onion, a 400 g can of drained and rinsed white beans or chickpeas, 185 ml of white wine, a heaped teaspoon of smoked paprika, a few thyme sprigs and 6 boneless, skinless chicken thighs in a roasting tin. Season and drizzle over some olive oil. Mix and rest the chicken on top of the vegetables. Bake at 180°C for 1 hour.

4. Combine a finely chopped onion, 500 g mince, spices of your choice, a 400 g can of drained and rinsed kidney beans and a 400 g can of whole peeled tomatoes in a sauté pan and cook over medium–low heat for 20 minutes. Add a few handfuls of leafy greens and 250 g of leftover cooked rice and mix to warm through. Serve with Greek yoghurt and avocado wedges.

5. For a fast meatball soup, shape 500 g of chicken mince, an egg, chopped dill and a handful of parmesan and breadcrumbs into walnut-sized balls. Poach in chicken stock or broth until cooked through. Add softened noodles of your choice.

6. For a quick fish curry, pour a 400 ml can of coconut milk into a sauté pan. Add a pinch of ground turmeric, 1 teaspoon each of grated ginger and lemongrass, the grated zest of 1 lime and 3 coriander stalks. Season with salt and bring to a simmer. Add bite-sized chunks of salmon or firm white fish and poach for 5–8 minutes. Serve with rice.

7. To revamp leftover schnitzel, heat a little olive oil in a frying pan over medium heat. Add a chopped onion and garlic clove and a pinch of chilli flakes. Fry until the onion is softened. Add a handful or two of frozen peas and two 400 g cans of crushed tomatoes. Season and cook for 15 minutes. Add the leftover cooked schnitzel and warm through. Serve with crusty bread.

8. Combine 100 g of chopped smoked salmon, 200 g of drained canned salmon, 100 g of crème fraîche or sour cream, grated zest of 1 lemon, a small handful of dill fronds and flat-leaf parsley leaves, some baby capers, chopped cornichons and a pinch of cayenne pepper. Mix well and season. Dress a bowl of lettuce leaves with a little lemon juice and top with mounds of the salmon mixture and crunchy croutons, or simply serve as a dip with cucumber batons and crackers.

CHICKEN NOODLE SOUP

Chicken noodle soup always reminds me of home. It's hard not to be sentimental about it when it evokes memories of Mum cooking her version and that wonderful aroma filling the house on wet winter days. Mum and I prepare our soups in slightly different ways. I use roasted chicken wings as they're inexpensive, full of flavour, and high in collagen, which makes for an extra-restorative result.

SERVES: 8   PREP: 15 MINUTES   COOK: 3 HOURS 25 MINUTES   SUITABLE TO FREEZE

1.5 kg chicken wings
1 tablespoon olive oil
1 onion, unpeeled and quartered
2 carrots, halved lengthways
2 celery stalks
1 garlic bulb, halved horizontally
1 leek, sliced lengthways through the root (keep the root intact), washed well
3 fresh bay leaves, 1 small handful of thyme and 3 flat-leaf parsley sprigs, tied together with kitchen string
1 teaspoon black peppercorns
salt flakes
1 nest vermicelli egg pasta

Preheat the oven to 200°C.

Place the chicken wings in a large baking tray and evenly drizzle over the oil. Rub in well with your hands, then roast for 40–45 minutes, tossing halfway through, until golden brown.

Transfer the roasted chicken wings to a stockpot. Completely cover with water and bring to the boil, skimming off the impurities that rise to the surface. When the broth is clear, add the vegetables, herbs, peppercorns and a small pinch of salt. Reduce the heat to low and simmer gently for 2–2 ½ hours.

Strain the broth through a fine sieve into a large saucepan. Reserve the vegetables and chicken wings and set aside to cool a little. When cool enough to handle, pick the meat from the chicken bones (discard the bones and any fat) and place in a bowl. Cut all the vegetables into bite-sized pieces and add to the bowl with the meat. Discard the herbs, peppercorns and garlic.

Add the chicken and vegetables to the broth and bring to the boil. Add the vermicelli and cook until al dente. Spoon into bowls and serve.

 To freeze, transfer the soup to a large container or bowl, ensuring the chicken and vegetables are submerged in the broth, and place in the fridge overnight. The next day, skim off the layer of fat that has solidified on the surface. Portion the soup into containers and freeze for up to 3 months.

If freezing, don't add the pasta until you thaw and reheat the soup in a saucepan.

PANTRY STAPLES
Black peppercorns
Carrots
Garlic
Olive oil
Onion
Salt
Vermicelli egg pasta

SHOPPING LIST
Celery
Chicken wings
Fresh bay leaves
Fresh flat-leaf parsley
Fresh thyme
Leek

COUSCOUS ROYALE

Couscous Royale is a much-loved celebratory dish from North Africa. It's great for dinner parties or if you're looking to batch cook and freeze portions. A family friend who lives in Morocco cooked this amazing dish for me and I fell completely in love. Traditionally, it's prepared with seven varieties of vegetable, many spices and chicken and red meat, including merguez sausages, but I've modified the recipe to make it much simpler.

**SERVES: 4–6   PREP: 20 MINUTES, PLUS OVERNIGHT SOAKING
COOK: 2 HOURS 30 MINUTES   SUITABLE TO FREEZE**

100 g dried chickpeas
2 tablespoons olive oil
1.5 kg boned lamb shoulder, excess fat removed, cut into 4 pieces
4 chicken drumsticks
salt flakes and freshly ground black pepper
2 onions, chopped
1 tablespoon ras el hanout
pinch of saffron threads
2 teaspoons harissa paste
2 tablespoons tomato paste
2 carrots, cut into 3 cm chunks
1 turnip, quartered
1 litre chicken stock
2 zucchini, cut into 3 cm chunks
½ small savoy cabbage, core intact, halved
500 g (about 2 ½ cups) instant couscous
20 g butter

Soak the chickpeas in water overnight, then rinse and drain.

Drizzle 1 tablespoon of oil over the lamb and chicken and season generously with salt and pepper.

Heat a large frying pan over medium–high heat, add the lamb and chicken, in batches, and cook until golden all over.

Heat the remaining oil in a stockpot over medium heat, add the onion and sauté for 2–3 minutes to soften. Stir in the ras el hanout and saffron and cook for 30 seconds, then add the harissa and tomato paste and cook for a further 2 minutes. Add the lamb and chicken and stir to coat in the spiced onion mix, then add the carrot, turnip and chickpeas. Pour in the stock and enough water to cover and season with salt. Bring to the boil, then reduce the heat to low, partially cover the pot with a lid and simmer for 45 minutes. Add the zucchini and cabbage and cook for a further 1–1 ¼ hours until the lamb is almost falling apart and the chickpeas are tender.

Place the couscous in a large heatproof bowl and add a pinch of salt and the butter. Bring 750 ml (3 cups) of water to the boil in a kettle, pour over the couscous and immediately cover with plastic wrap. Set aside to steam for 5–10 minutes, then, using a fork, gently scratch the surface to separate and fluff the grains.

Mound the couscous onto a large platter. Using a slotted spoon, drain the vegetables and place on top of the couscous, then add the meat and cover with foil to keep warm.

Bring the broth to the boil and cook for 8–10 minutes to concentrate the flavours a little. Spoon a few ladlefuls of the aromatic broth over the meat, vegetables and couscous and serve in the middle of the table.

* Freeze any leftover broth. It's a great base for any soup or stew.

If you can't find ras el hanout, make your own by combining 1 teaspoon each of ground ginger, cumin, coriander, cinnamon, paprika and turmeric.

PANTRY STAPLES
Butter
Carrots
Chicken stock
Couscous
Dried chickpeas
Harissa paste
Olive oil
Onions
Ras el hanout
Saffron
Salt and pepper
Tomato paste

SHOPPING LIST
Chicken drumsticks
Lamb shoulder
Savoy cabbage
Turnip
Zucchini

DAD'S CURRIED SAUSAGES

Before starting this book, I asked my friends and family what childhood dishes they still love. Among the usual suspects featured curried sausages, bringing back many weeknight dinner memories. I think a lot of Australian families dished up this old-fashioned favourite because it was quick to make, inexpensive and freezer friendly. I'm sharing my dad's recipe. He likes to think of himself as a curried sausages expert ... I'll give him that glory, as his version is pretty delicious. Serve with a side of steamed rice.

SERVES: 4   PREP: 10 MINUTES   COOK: 50 MINUTES

800 g thick beef or pork sausages
1 tablespoon vegetable oil
1 onion, sliced
3 cm piece of ginger, finely chopped
1 small handful of coriander sprigs, leaves picked, stalks finely chopped
1 teaspoon cumin seeds
1 tablespoon curry powder
2 large tomatoes, diced (or 1 x 400 g can whole peeled tomatoes, drained)
300 ml beef or chicken stock
1 small sweet potato, cut into 2 cm cubes
salt flakes and freshly ground black pepper
1 x 270 ml can coconut milk, reserve a few tablespoons to serve
4 kale leaves, central stalk removed, leaves roughly chopped

Bring a large saucepan of water to a gentle simmer, add the sausages and poach for 4–5 minutes. Drain and set aside until cool enough to handle. Slice the sausages into 3 cm pieces.

Heat the oil in a large sauté pan over medium–high heat, add the onion, ginger and coriander stalks and cook for 3–4 minutes until softened. Stir in the cumin seeds, followed by the curry powder and cook for about 1 minute until fragrant. Add the tomato and cook for 2–3 minutes until it has broken down to form a thick paste. Pour in the stock and, using a wooden spoon, scrape the bottom of the pan to detach any caramelised bits. Bring back to the boil, then add the sweet potato and season with salt and pepper.

Pour the coconut milk into the pan and stir through. Reduce the heat to medium–low and simmer for 10–12 minutes. Add the sausage and cook for a further 15–20 minutes until the sauce is thick and rich and the sweet potato is tender. Add the kale and cook for 3 minutes until it has just wilted. Drizzle on the reserved coconut milk, scatter over the coriander leaves and serve with some steamed rice.

PANTRY STAPLES
Beef or chicken stock
Beef or pork sausages
Coconut milk
Cumin seeds
Curry powder
Fresh ginger
Onion
Salt and pepper
Vegetable oil

SHOPPING LIST
Fresh coriander
Kale
Sweet potato
Tomatoes

ITALIAN PORK IN MILK

This truly wonderful dish – I would go so far as to say it's one of my all-time favourites – comes from Emilia-Romagna in northern Italy. I know pork braised in milk sounds bizarre, but I can assure you this cooking method has been around for centuries. The lactic acid in the milk tenderises the meat, making it incredibly succulent. Traditionally, a leaner cut like pork loin roast is used, but I like pork neck as it doesn't dry out. Serve with baked rice or pappardelle. Delizioso!

SERVES: 4   PREP: 10 MINUTES   COOK: 2 HOURS 15 MINUTES

1 x 700 g piece of pork scotch
   fillet (pork neck)
salt flakes and freshly ground
   black pepper
1 tablespoon olive oil
1 onion, sliced
4 sage sprigs
3 garlic cloves, bruised
2 cloves
1 wide strip of lemon peel
250 ml (1 cup) white wine (such as
   chardonnay or sauvignon blanc)
700 ml milk
50 g (⅓ cup) whole almonds,
   toasted

PANTRY STAPLES
Almonds
Cloves
Garlic
Lemon
Milk
Olive oil
Onion
Salt and pepper
White wine

SHOPPING LIST
Fresh sage
Pork scotch fillet

Preheat the oven to 160°C.

Season the pork with salt and pepper.

Heat the oil in a large ovenproof sauté pan, add the pork and seal on all sides. Remove the pork and set aside.

Add the onion to the pan and sauté for a few minutes to soften before adding the sage, garlic, cloves, lemon peel and wine. Bring to the boil and cook for 1 minute, then return the pork, pour on the milk and season with a little salt. Cover with baking paper cut to fit and a tight-fitting lid and transfer to the oven to cook for 2 hours, turning the pork halfway through. The pork is ready when it's soft and can be pulled apart easily. Remove the pork from the pan and place on a chopping board.

Discard the lemon peel, cloves and sage stalks, leaving the sage leaves in the pan. Bring the sauce to the boil and cook until reduced by one-third.

Shred the pork, place back in the sauce and toss through. Scatter over the almonds and serve.

KOREAN-STYLE CRISPY PORK BELLY

Looking for a sure-fire way to take your roast pork to the next level? Inspired by the flavours of kimchi, soy sauce and apple juice, this dish is an incredible marriage of sweet, salty, spicy and savoury with deliciously tender meat and super-crispy crackling. Just remember to get a good-quality piece of pork, air-dry the skin for the best crackling and ensure the flesh is completely submerged in the liquid while cooking.

SERVES: 4   PREP: 10 MINUTES, PLUS OVERNIGHT AIR-DRYING   COOK: 3 HOURS

1 x 1.5 kg pork belly, skin scored
1 tablespoon vegetable oil
salt flakes
375 ml (1 ½ cups) apple juice
125 ml (½ cup) light soy sauce
125 ml (½ cup) black vinegar
1 onion, roughly chopped
2 garlic cloves, bruised
3 cm piece of ginger,
    roughly chopped
150 g kimchi, plus extra to serve

To air-dry the pork, place it uncovered on a tray and transfer to the fridge overnight. Remove the pork from the fridge 1 hour before cooking.

Preheat the oven to 220°C.

Rub the oil all over the pork and season with salt. Place the pork, skin-side up, in a baking dish and roast for 15–20 minutes until the skin turns golden and begins to blister.

In a jug, mix together the apple juice, soy sauce, vinegar and 375 ml (1 ½ cups) of water.

Remove the pork from the oven and reduce the temperature to 160°C. Place the pork on a plate and set aside. Carefully add the onion, garlic, ginger and kimchi to the baking dish (it will be very hot) and, using a wooden spoon, stir to ensure the vegetables soften and get a little colour. (There's no need to put the dish over heat, the residual heat will do the work.) Pour in the apple juice mixture and evenly spread out the vegetables. Return the pork belly, skin-side up, to the dish, ensuring none of the crackling touches the liquid. Ideally, you want just the flesh to be submerged.

Return the dish to the oven and roast for 2–2 ½ hours, adding a little water if the sauce reduces too much. If the crackling is getting too much colour, loosely cover the dish with foil. Remove from the oven and transfer the pork to a chopping board. Rest in a warm place for 20 minutes.

Thickly slice the pork and serve with the onion and kimchi sauce and some extra kimchi on the side.

✻ I also like to serve this with sliced cucumbers and steamed rice.

PANTRY STAPLES   **SHOPPING LIST**
Black vinegar   Apple juice
Fresh ginger   Pork belly
Garlic
Kimchi
Light soy sauce
Onion
Salt
Vegetable oil

LEEK AND HAM SOUP POT PIE

This is not your average soup as I've glammed it up by covering it in flaky puff pastry. It's the perfect winter warmer filled with smoky ham hock and sweet leek. What I love most about this recipe is the waft of aromatic goodness that greets you when you break into the buttery pastry, and the element of surprise when you discover the gooey cheese. So dramatic, so tasty!

SERVES: 4　PREP: 20 MINUTES, PLUS 30 MINUTES COOLING　COOK: 2 HOURS

2 tablespoons olive oil

2 large leeks, white and pale green part only, finely sliced

450 g desiree potatoes, cut into 1 cm dice

1 smoked ham hock (about 800 g)

2 litres chicken stock (ideally homemade, otherwise use salt-reduced)

1 small handful of thyme, leaves picked

2 fresh bay leaves

plain flour, for dusting

375 g frozen butter puff pastry, thawed, plus more if required (see Note)

freshly ground black pepper

80 g cheddar, coarsely grated

1 egg, whisked

You will need four 650 ml ovenproof soup bowls for this recipe.

Heat the oil in a large saucepan over medium heat. Add the leek and cook, stirring frequently, for 4–5 minutes until softened. Add the potato, ham hock, stock, thyme and bay leaves and bring to the boil, skimming off any impurities that rise to the surface. Reduce the heat to low, cover and gently simmer for 1½ hours until the meat falls easily from the bone.

While the soup is cooking, prepare the pastry lids. Roll out the pastry on a lightly floured surface. Using the rim of one of your soup bowls as a guide, cut out four squares of pastry that are 3 cm wider than the rim. Cut a 2 cm circle from the centre of each pastry square and discard (or save for another use). Place the cut-out pastry squares between sheets of baking paper, transfer to a plate and chill in the fridge until required.

Preheat the oven to 200°C.

Remove the hock and herbs from the soup and, when cool enough to handle, shred the meat, discarding the skin, fat and bone. Return the meat to the soup and season with pepper – it probably won't need any salt, as the hock and stock should be salty enough. Allow the soup to cool slightly for 30 minutes.

Divide the soup among the bowls, ensuring you only three-quarters fill them, and sprinkle on the cheese. Brush the egg around the rim of each bowl and drape a cut-out pastry square over the top. Press the pastry to the side of the bowl and brush with more egg wash. Place the soup pots on a baking tray and bake for 20–25 minutes until the pastry is golden and cooked through.

* The amount of pastry you will need depends on the diameter of the bowls you use.

Don't worry if the pastry sinks at the beginning of cooking – it will come back up again.

This makes four generous serves. If you want to make more smaller pies, ensure that you only three-quarter fill the bowls so the pastry doesn't touch the soup when placed in the oven.

PANTRY STAPLES

Cheddar
Chicken stock
Egg
Frozen butter puff pastry
Olive oil
Pepper
Plain flour
Potatoes

SHOPPING LIST

Fresh bay leaves
Fresh thyme
Leeks
Smoked ham hock

FENNEL SOUP

Fennel is renowned for its versatility – and with good reason, as it can be prepared in so many ways, raw and cooked. Here, I use it as a hero in the most delicate and silky-smooth soup. Be sure not to get too much colour on the vegetables; the aim is to show off the lovely white of the fennel. I like to add a teaspoon of coriander seeds to give the final result a nutty, citrussy note that works nicely with the anise flavour of the fennel.

SERVES: 4   PREP: 15 MINUTES   COOK: 30 MINUTES   SUITABLE TO FREEZE

3 fennel bulbs, trimmed, a few
  fronds reserved to serve
15 g butter
1 tablespoon olive oil, plus extra
  to serve
1 onion, chopped
1 teaspoon ground coriander
2 desiree potatoes, quartered
salt flakes
freshly shaved parmesan, to serve
freshly ground black pepper

PANTRY STAPLES   **SHOPPING LIST**
Butter   Fennel
Ground coriander
Olive oil
Onion
Parmesan
Potatoes
Salt and pepper

Cut each fennel bulb into four even wedges.

Heat the butter and oil in a large saucepan, add the onion, fennel and ground coriander and toss. Cook, without colouring the onion or fennel, for 2–3 minutes. Pour in enough water to completely cover, then add the potato, season with salt and bring to the boil. Reduce the heat to medium–low and cook for 20–25 minutes until the potato is soft.

Remove the pan from the heat and blend the soup with a hand-held blender until smooth. Taste and add more salt if required, then portion into shallow bowls. Sprinkle over the reserved fennel fronds and the parmesan, drizzle on a little extra olive oil and finish with a grind of pepper.

HARIRA

This traditional Moroccan soup is eaten mostly at sundown during Ramadan to break the fast. For that reason, it's renowned for being a super-nourishing and hearty dish. When I learned to make this in Marrakesh, the chefs added pieces of lamb shoulder for a more filling soup. I like to serve this as a simple, satisfying dinner during the cooler months.

SERVES: 4–6   **PREP:** 15 MINUTES   **COOK:** 1 HOUR 35 MINUTES   **SUITABLE TO FREEZE**

2 tablespoons olive oil
1 onion, diced
2 celery stalks, finely chopped
1 small pinch of saffron threads
½ teaspoon each of ground ginger, cumin and turmeric
5 coriander sprigs, stalks and leaves finely chopped, plus extra to serve
5 flat-leaf parsley sprigs, stalks and leaves finely chopped, plus extra to serve
95 g (½ cup) brown lentils
180 g dried chickpeas
1 tablespoon tomato paste
1 x 400 g can whole peeled tomatoes, crushed
salt flakes and freshly ground black pepper

Heat the oil in a large, heavy-based saucepan over medium heat, add the onion and celery and cook for 2–3 minutes to soften. Add the spices and cook for 1 minute, then stir in the herbs and cook for a further 1 minute. Add the lentils, chickpeas and tomato paste and cook for another minute before adding the tomatoes and enough water to cover 3 cm above the surface (about 2–3 litres). Season with salt and pepper and bring to the boil. Reduce the heat to low, cover with the lid and cook for 1½–2 hours until the lentils and chickpeas are tender.

Portion the soup into serving bowls and serve sprinkled with the extra herbs.

 If you'd like to add lamb to this dish, use 250 g diced lamb shoulder and stir it in after the onions and celery.

PANTRY STAPLES
Brown lentils
Canned whole peeled tomatoes
Dried chickpeas
Ground cumin
Ground ginger
Ground turmeric
Olive oil
Onion
Saffron
Salt and pepper
Tomato paste

SHOPPING LIST
Celery
Fresh coriander
Fresh parsley

SLOW-COOKED BEEF SHORT RIBS

The combination of malty full-bodied beer, salty soy sauce and sweet honey is a magical thing. This holy trinity adds an incredible depth of flavour to these slow-cooked ribs, reducing down to form a savoury caramel-like sauce. These ribs are wonderful served with rice and shredded cabbage or steamed greens. Alternatively, steam some bao buns (available in the freezer section at Asian grocers) and serve the meat shredded with kimchi, cucumber and sliced spring onion.

SERVES: 4–6   PREP: 15 MINUTES   COOK: 3 HOURS 15 MINUTES

330 ml dark ale
160 g honey
125 ml (½ cup) soy sauce
500 ml (2 cups) beef or
  chicken stock
6 meaty beef short ribs
  (about 350 g each)
1 onion, chopped
4 coriander sprigs, leaves picked,
  stalks and roots reserved
3 star anise

Preheat the oven to 160°C.

Combine the beer, honey, soy sauce and stock in a bowl and mix well.

Place the ribs in a large roasting tin in a single layer, then add the onion and coriander stalks and roots. Pour the beer mixture over the ribs and add the star anise. Cover the tin with baking paper and two sheets of foil and bake for 2½–3 hours until the meat falls away from the bones easily. Carefully transfer the ribs to a tray lined with foil and spoon over a little of the cooking liquid.

Strain the remaining juices in the tin into a saucepan and cook over low heat, skimming off any oil that rises to the surface, for 10–15 minutes until reduced by half.

Place the ribs on a platter, pour over the sauce and scatter on the coriander leaves.

 If you have a pressure cooker, seal the meat and onion first, then pour in the liquid and cook under pressure for 45 minutes. Carefully remove the ribs and reduce the sauce by one-third until thick and rich.

If you have a slow cooker, seal the meat and onion, pour in the liquid, cover with the lid and cook for 8 hours. Reduce the sauce by one-third in a saucepan once the meat is cooked.

This dish can be made up to 3 days ahead. Once the ribs come out of the oven, arrange them on a tray, cover and refrigerate. Place the sauce in a bowl, cool to room temperature and place, uncovered, in the fridge. The next day you'll notice all the fat has come to the surface and solidified. Scoop off the fat with a spoon and then cook the sauce until reduced. This is the best way to prepare the sauce and gives the glossiest results.

PANTRY STAPLES

Beef or chicken
  stock
Honey
Onion
Soy sauce
Star anise

SHOPPING LIST

Beef short ribs
Dark ale
Fresh coriander

SWEET

APPLE SLIPPERS

These flaky little apple-filled pastries remind of my mémé. When I went to France to spend my holidays with her as a little girl, we would walk to the boulangerie every day to get our bread and each time, without fail, I would throw a mini tantrum (my poor grandmother!) when I wasn't allowed to get a chausson aux pomme (apple slipper). Thankfully, I can now make a big batch for myself, so there are fewer tantrums. The name apple slippers comes from the shape of the filled pastry, which looks like the tip of a slipper.

MAKES: 9   PREP: 30 MINUTES, PLUS 1 HOUR CHILLING   COOK: 1 HOUR

700 g granny smith apples
   (about 4), peeled, cored and
   cut into 5 mm chunks
3 tablespoons caster sugar
finely grated zest and juice of
   ½ lemon
1½ teaspoons ground cinnamon
3 sheets frozen puff pastry, thawed
1 egg yolk, lightly whisked
3 tablespoons apricot jam

Combine the apple, sugar, lemon zest and juice and cinnamon in a saucepan and add 1 tablespoon of water. Cover and cook over medium heat for 10–15 minutes until softened. Transfer half the apple mixture to a jug and puree with a hand-held blender, then fold into the rest of the cooked apple. Set aside to cool completely.

Grease and line two baking trays with baking paper.

Cut three 11 cm rounds from each sheet of pastry and place on the prepared trays. Brush around the side with a little whisked egg yolk. Divide the cooked apple among the pastry rounds, placing mounds in the centre. Fold the pastry over the apple to form a half-moon shape and lightly press with a cupped hand to remove any air bubbles. Press around the cut side of the pastry with your hand to seal. Brush the top with a little more whisked egg yolk and chill in the fridge for 1 hour to set the egg wash.

Preheat the oven to 200°C.

Using a skewer or small paring knife, score the apple slippers on the diagonal following the half-moon shape. Bake for 10 minutes until beginning to puff, then reduce the temperature to 180°C and bake for a further 25–30 minutes until puffed and a deep golden colour.

Melt the apricot jam in a saucepan. While the pastries are still hot, brush with the jam to glaze. Cool to room temperature and serve.

PANTRY STAPLES   **SHOPPING LIST**

Apples
Apricot jam
Caster sugar
Egg
Frozen puff pastry
Ground cinnamon
Lemon

MORELLO CHERRY BREAD-AND-BUTTER PUDDING

In the spirit of the weeknight theme of this book, a good old bread-and-butter pudding had to be included. Dad would often make this with leftover bread as a treat in the middle of the week. I've used morello cherries, but it's just as delicious with other jarred or canned fruits, such as apricots or plums.

SERVES: 4   PREP: 30 MINUTES, PLUS 30 MINUTES STANDING   COOK: 1 HOUR

5 egg yolks
220 g (1 cup) sugar
600 ml thickened cream,
    plus extra to serve
1 teaspoon vanilla extract
grated zest of 1 lemon
¼ teaspoon ground cinnamon
butter, for greasing
1 x 500 g brioche loaf, crusts
    removed, cut into 10 slices,
    then halved into triangles
1 x 670 g jar pitted morello cherries,
    drained, liquid reserved
2 tablespoons demerara sugar

Whisk the egg yolks and half the sugar in a heatproof bowl until pale and thick.

Combine the cream, vanilla, lemon zest and cinnamon in a saucepan and bring just to the boil. Slowly whisk into the egg mixture until smooth, then set the custard aside until required.

Grease a 1.5 litre baking dish with butter.

Arrange half the brioche in the prepared dish, making sure it comes up the side and pressing down to compact. Add half the cherries, then arrange the remaining brioche, buttered-side up, on top, followed by the remaining cherries. Little by little, pour over the custard, allowing the bread to absorb the liquid. Leave the pudding to stand for at least 30 minutes, so the custard soaks into the brioche.

Meanwhile, combine the reserved cherry liquid and the remaining sugar in a saucepan and bring to the boil, stirring to dissolve the sugar. Reduce the heat to medium and cook for 12–15 minutes until reduced by half to a sticky syrup.

Preheat the oven to 160°C.

Sprinkle the demerara sugar over the pudding and bake for 35–40 minutes until golden and set, covering with foil if the pudding is getting too dark on top. Serve with a spoonful of the cherry syrup and a drizzle of cream.

PANTRY STAPLES

Butter
Eggs
Ground cinnamon
Lemon
Sugar
Thickened cream
Vanilla extract

SHOPPING LIST

Brioche
Demerara sugar
Morello cherries

AMANDINE TART WITH SPICED APRICOTS

This tart is very easy to make and is sure to impress. The base, a simple shortcrust pastry that doesn't need to be blind-baked, is filled with a nutty almond cream perfumed with a hint of brandy. Almonds and apricots are best friends, and a quick poached dried apricot compote on the side works perfectly here. I always make sure I have almond meal and dried apricots in the pantry to whip up this tart. And I love it when there is a leftover slice or two, as it's absolutely delicious the next day with my morning coffee.

SERVES: 8   PREP: 40 MINUTES, PLUS 1 HOUR CHILLING   COOK: 1 HOUR 10 MINUTES

225 g (1 ½ cups) plain flour
pinch of salt flakes
100 g cold butter, cubed,
  plus extra for greasing
5 eggs
300 g caster sugar
1 vanilla pod, split and scraped
1 cinnamon stick
4 cloves
2 wide strips of orange peel
200 g dried apricots
200 g crème fraîche, plus extra
  to serve
2 tablespoons brandy or dark rum
160 g almond meal
40 g (½ cup) flaked almonds,
  toasted

Place the flour, salt, butter and one egg in a food processor and pulse until a fine crumb forms. Add 2–3 tablespoons of water and pulse again. (You can also do this by hand if you prefer. Simply rub the flour into the butter, egg and water until the mixture becomes crumbly.) Tip onto a lightly floured work surface and knead two or three times to bring the dough together. Press into a disc shape, cover with plastic wrap and refrigerate for 1 hour.

Place 500 ml (2 cups) of water, 100 g of sugar, the vanilla pod (save the seeds for later), spices and orange peel in a saucepan and bring to the boil. Add the apricots, then reduce the heat to low and simmer for 30 minutes. Remove from the heat and cool to room temperature. (This can be made up to a week ahead and stored in an airtight container in the fridge.)

Preheat the oven to 180°C. Grease a 26 cm round tart tin with a detachable base with a little butter.

Roll out the dough on a lightly floured surface until 2–3 mm thick and 2–3 cm wider than the tart tin. Line the tin with the pastry and trim the excess. Carefully press the pastry into the side of the tin to remove any air bubbles. It's okay if the pastry sits a little higher than the rim, as it will shrink slightly when it cooks. Place the lined tart tin on a tray and transfer to the fridge to chill while you make the filling.

Combine the remaining eggs, sugar and the vanilla seeds in a bowl and whisk until the sugar has dissolved. Whisk in the crème fraîche, brandy or rum and almond meal.

Remove the pastry shell from the fridge and pour in the almond filling. Bake for 30–35 minutes until the top is a deep golden colour. Remove and, while still hot, delicately brush on a thin layer of glaze from the spiced apricots. Set aside to cool.

Remove the tart from the tin and brush with some more of the apricot glaze. Spoon over the apricots and vanilla pod, then sprinkle with the flaked almonds. Slice and serve with a dollop of crème fraîche.

PANTRY STAPLES   **SHOPPING LIST**

Almond meal   Orange
Brandy or dark rum
Butter
Caster sugar
Cinnamon stick
Cloves
Crème fraîche
Dried apricots
Eggs
Flaked almonds
Plain flour
Salt
Vanilla pod

STICKY SAVARIN BUNS

These buns are essentially the French take on the classic rum baba, a yeast-risen cake similar to brioche in texture and flavour. What makes them so special and so appetising is that they are soaked in rum. They're definitely an adult dessert. Instead of using a traditional mould, which can be hard to come by, I bake mine in a muffin tin. The results are just as good.

MAKES: 12   PREP: 30 MINUTES, PLUS 1 HOUR PROVING   COOK: 20 MINUTES

150 g butter, cubed and softened,
    plus extra for greasing
2 teaspoons (7 g sachet) dried
    instant yeast
1½ tablespoons lukewarm water
500 g (3⅓ cups) plain flour,
    plus extra for dusting
pinch of salt flakes
3 tablespoons caster sugar
3 eggs
125 ml (½ cup) milk
185 ml (¾ cup) dark rum
115 g (⅓ cup) honey
1 egg, lightly whisked
double cream, to serve
2 mangoes, cheeks sliced
pulp of 2 passionfruit

PANTRY STAPLES   **SHOPPING LIST**

Butter   Mangoes
Caster sugar   Passionfruit
Cream
Dark rum
Eggs
Honey
Instant yeast
Milk
Plain flour
Salt

Grease a standard (80 ml) 12-hole muffin tin with butter.

Combine the yeast and water in a small bowl and stir to dissolve the yeast. Transfer to the bowl of an electric mixer fitted with the dough hook, add the flour, salt, sugar, eggs and milk and knead on medium speed until a sticky dough forms. Now add the butter a few cubes at a time and mix on medium–low speed for a minute each time until the butter is incorporated and a smooth, soft dough begins to form.

Flour a clean work surface, scrape the dough out of the bowl (it will be a bit sticky) and portion into twelve pieces. Flour your hands and gently roll the dough into smooth balls. Place in the prepared muffin tin. Cover with a clean tea towel and set aside in a warm spot for 1 hour until the dough has almost doubled in size.

Preheat the oven to 180°C.

Place the rum and honey in a saucepan and bring to the boil, then remove from the heat.

Brush the tops of the buns with the egg and bake for 15 minutes until golden. Remove from the oven and, while still hot, pierce the buns all over with a skewer. Pour the honey mixture evenly over each bun and allow it to soak in. Set aside to cool in the tin.

Serve each savarin bun with a dollop of cream, a few slices of mango and some passionfruit.

YOGHURT PANNA COTTA

I love this recipe to bits, it's my favourite in this chapter. It's also the simplest and, for me, the tastiest, as it's tangy and creamy yet super light – the perfect way to end a meal. The panna cotta can be made a few days in advance, so if I'm having a dinner party, it's my go-to dessert. I'm not keen on making individual panna cottas; instead, I love setting the mixture in a deep tray and scooping out portions. It's rustic, and that's what makes it so beautiful.

SERVES: 8   PREP: 10 MINUTES, PLUS 5 HOURS CHILLING   COOK: 10 MINUTES

300 ml cream
100 g caster sugar, plus
   2 tablespoons extra
3 cardamom pods, bruised
1 teaspoon vanilla extract
2½ titanium-strength gelatine
   leaves, soaked in cold water
   for 10 minutes
800 g Greek yoghurt
500 g strawberries, hulled
   and quartered
grated zest and juice of 1 orange

PANTRY STAPLES
Cardamom pods
Caster sugar
Cream
Gelatine leaves
Greek yoghurt
Vanilla extract

SHOPPING LIST
Orange
Strawberries

Combine the cream, sugar, cardamom and vanilla in a saucepan and bring to the boil. Remove from the heat and set aside to steep for 10 minutes.

Reheat the cream mixture and bring to a simmer, then remove from the heat. Squeeze the excess water from the gelatine, add to the cream mixture and mix until it has dissolved. Cool a little, then strain into a large bowl and whisk in the yoghurt until well incorporated. Transfer to a 1.5 litre capacity deep tray. Carefully place a piece of plastic wrap over the tray, ensuring it doesn't touch the panna cotta mixture. Chill in the fridge for 5 hours or, even better, overnight.

Combine the strawberries, orange zest and juice and the extra 2 tablespoons of sugar. Macerate at room temperature for 2–3 hours.

To serve, scoop a generous dollop of the panna cotta onto plates and serve with the strawberry salad.

* Get the most flavour out of the strawberries by leaving them at room temperature.

BUTTERSCOTCH APPLES WITH CINNAMON CRUMBLE

Here, I've taken the concept of apple crumble, jazzed it up and given it a modern twist by serving the apple whole with lashings of butterscotch sauce. This is the perfect dessert after a Sunday roast, and it's super easy to make.

MAKES: 6   PREP: 30 MINUTES   COOK: 55 MINUTES

30 g butter
160 g brown sugar
250 ml (1 cup) thickened cream
3 tablespoons quick oats
125 g blanched hazelnuts
   (or any nut of your choice),
   finely chopped
2 tablespoons sesame seeds
¾ teaspoon ground cinnamon
6 granny smith or pink lady apples
vanilla ice cream, to serve

Preheat the oven to 180°C. Line a baking tray with baking paper.

Place 20 g of butter, the sugar and cream in a saucepan and bring to the boil, stirring regularly. Cook for 3–4 minutes until smooth and glossy. Remove the butterscotch sauce from the heat.

Combine the oats, nuts, sesame seeds and cinnamon in a bowl, pour over 3 tablespoons of butterscotch sauce and mix into sticky clusters. Roughly spread out on the prepared tray and bake for 12–15 minutes until golden and crisp. Allow the crumble to cool to room temperature.

Meanwhile, place the apples in a baking dish large enough to fit them all. Dot the remaining butter on top of the apples and bake for 20 minutes. Remove from the oven and pour the remaining butterscotch sauce around the apples. Bake for a further 20–30 minutes until the apples are tender when pierced with a skewer. Allow to cool for 5–10 minutes (the butterscotch will be very hot).

To serve, place an apple on each serving plate and spoon over a generous amount of butterscotch sauce. Add a pile of crumble and serve with a scoop of ice cream.

PANTRY STAPLES
Apples
Brown sugar
Butter
Cream
Ground cinnamon
Hazelnuts
Quick oats
Sesame seeds

SHOPPING LIST
Vanilla ice cream

COCONUT RICE PUDDING WITH PINEAPPLE COMPOTE

Rice pudding is one of those versatile sweet dishes that can be enjoyed either at breakfast or for a quick dessert. I love this tropical twist, as it's light and fresh. The best part about this is that you can change up the milk. If you need a dairy-free alternative, it's just as delicious with almond milk.

SERVES: 6   **PREP:** 15 MINUTES   **COOK:** 1 HOUR 15 MINUTES

½ pineapple (about 500 g), peeled
1 tablespoon finely grated ginger
220 g (1 cup) caster sugar
grated zest and juice of 2 limes,
   plus extra zest to serve
140 g (⅔ cup) arborio rice
750 ml (3 cups) milk
270 ml coconut milk
55 g (1 cup) flaked coconut, toasted
mint leaves, to serve

Coarsely grate the pineapple on a box grater into a large saucepan so all the juice is collected. Add the ginger and 250 ml (1 cup) of water, place over high heat and bring to the boil. Reduce the heat to medium–low and cook for 20–25 minutes until the pineapple has softened. Add 110 g (½ cup) of sugar and cook for a further 15–20 minutes until golden and thick. Stir in the lime zest and juice and set aside until required.

Place the rice in a saucepan and cover generously with water. Bring to the boil and par-cook for 2 minutes. Drain.

Pour the milk into a saucepan, bring to a gentle boil and add the par-cooked rice and half the coconut milk. Reduce the heat to low and cook, stirring often to avoid sticking, for 15–20 minutes until the rice is almost cooked. Add the remaining coconut milk and sugar and cook, stirring constantly, for a further 5 minutes until the mixture is thick and the rice is cooked through. Set aside for 10 minutes to allow it to thicken.

Spoon the warm rice pudding into shallow bowls or decorative glasses, top with the pineapple compote, flaked coconut, mint leaves and extra lime zest and serve.

 The pineapple compote and rice pudding can also be chilled and served cold or made ahead and stored in an airtight container in the fridge for up to 1 week.

This rice pudding is also great with your favourite store-bought jam, or even fresh fruit.

PANTRY STAPLES
Arborio rice
Caster sugar
Coconut milk
Flaked coconut
Fresh ginger
Milk

SHOPPING LIST
Fresh mint
Fresh pineapple
Limes

SHORT-CUT SWEETIES

1. Place 4 egg whites in the bowl of an electric mixer and whisk with a pinch of salt and 1 teaspoon of white vinegar until soft peaks form. Slowly rain in 220 g of caster sugar. Keep whisking until stiff peaks form (about 10 minutes). Shape into small meringue nests on trays lined with baking paper. Bake at 120°C for 45–60 minutes until crisp on the outside. Cool completely in the oven. Serve topped with whipped cream and fresh seasonal fruit.

2. For a Sicilian cassata nuda, combine 500 g of fresh, full-fat ricotta with 2 tablespoons of thickened cream, 2 tablespoons of icing sugar, grated zest of 1 orange, a handful of finely chopped dried fruit, 100 g of finely chopped dark chocolate and a handful of chopped nuts of your choice. Spoon into serving bowls and top with flaked nuts.

3. Try this quick and refreshing Moroccan dessert. Segment citrus fruit and arrange on plates. Whip cream with a pinch of ground cinnamon and icing sugar to taste, then fold through a few tablespoons of Greek yoghurt. Dollop on top of the fruit.

4. For an instant chocolate mousse, melt 200 g of dark chocolate. Cool a little. Add 100 ml of your best extra-virgin olive oil and incorporate with a metal spoon until glossy. Whisk 300 ml of cream until soft peaks form. Fold in one-third of the chocolate mixture. Follow with another one-third, then finally fold in the last third. The mixture will become thick and fluffy. Perfect as is, or with chopped hazelnuts or fresh berries.

5. Chop 750 g of hulled strawberries, then add 2 tablespoons of sugar and a sprig of mint. Macerate for 2 hours. Remove the mint and puree the sweetened strawberries. Strain through a fine sieve and portion into shallow bowls. Serve with chopped strawberries, whipped cream and mint sprigs.

6. For poached peaches, combine 230 g of caster sugar with 500 ml (2 cups) of water in a large saucepan and stir to dissolve the sugar. Add the peaches, ensuring the liquid completely covers them, 2 cinnamon sticks and 2 star anise and poach for 5 minutes. Turn off the heat and allow the peaches to cool in the sugar syrup. Great with pureed raspberries.

7. For quick chocolate cookies, whisk 80 g of chopped softened butter with 60 g of caster sugar in a bowl. Add an egg and 1 teaspoon of vanilla extract and mix until fluffy. Sift in 160 g of plain flour, 2 tablespoons of cocoa powder and a pinch of salt and mix. Shape the dough into a disc. Cover with plastic wrap and chill in the fridge for 1 hour. Roll out on a lightly floured surface, cut into cookies and place on a lined baking tray. Bake at 180°C for 8–10 minutes. Cool on the tray. Sandwich the cookies together with jam or a nut spread.

8. For a no-churn coconut and lime ice cream, whisk 200 ml of thickened cream to soft peaks and fold through 250 ml of condensed milk, 250 ml of coconut cream, 2 tablespoons of desiccated coconut and the grated zest of 1 lime. Pour into a 1 litre container, cover and freeze overnight.

PEDRO'S TIRAMISU

Meaning 'pick me up', tiramisu is the most famous Italian dessert of all time. Yet, for some reason, I never order it in a restaurant. I think I've been disappointed too many times by over-complicated or poorly executed versions. Oh, and no one makes tiramisu like my friend Pedro. His recipe is unrivalled – it's classic, homely and utterly delectable. The key to getting the perfect result is good-quality mascarpone. Shop around and, ideally, buy it from a deli.

SERVES: 6   PREP: 40 MINUTES, PLUS OVERNIGHT CHILLING

6 egg yolks
1 teaspoon vanilla extract
200 g caster sugar
750 g mascarpone, brought
    to room temperature
3 egg whites
500 ml (2 cups) freshly brewed
    coffee, brought to room
    temperature
3 tablespoons coffee liqueur
    (such as Tia Maria)
36 savoiardi biscuits
1 tablespoon cocoa powder

Place the egg yolks, vanilla and 100 g of sugar in the bowl of an electric mixer and whisk on medium speed until pale and thick. Now, little by little, add the mascarpone and lightly whisk through, taking care not to overwork the mixture or the mascarpone will split.

In a separate bowl, whisk the egg whites until frothy. Slowly rain in the remaining sugar and continue to whisk until stiff peaks form.

Add one-third of the egg-white mixture to the mascarpone mixture and fold in. Add another third and fold in, making sure the mixture stays light and fluffy. Fold in the remaining third.

Spread a thin layer (about ½ cup) of mascarpone mixture over the base of a 30 cm x 20 cm serving dish.

Combine the coffee and liqueur in a shallow dish and, working in batches, dip in the biscuits, allowing each side to absorb the liquid. Arrange the biscuits side by side in the dish, ensuring all the mascarpone mixture is covered, then spread over half the remaining mascarpone mixture. Repeat with another batch of coffee liqueur–soaked biscuits and the remaining mascarpone. Using a fine sieve, dust the cocoa powder over the top and chill in the fridge overnight before serving.

PANTRY STAPLES

Caster sugar
Cocoa powder
Coffee
Coffee liqueur
Eggs
Vanilla extract

SHOPPING LIST

Mascarpone
Savoiardi biscuits

LEMONADE SCONE CAKE

There are many ways to make scones, but I always come back to this simple recipe that my Aunty Iris follows. The combination of lemonade and cream may seem unusual, but it creates a beautifully tender scone crumb. You can shape these the traditional way or put a spin on it, as I've done here, and make it into a double-decker cake. It's a real show stopper, perfect for your next afternoon tea.

SERVES: 8 **PREP:** 15 MINUTES **COOK:** 30 MINUTES

butter, for greasing
450 g (3 cups) self-raising flour,
   sifted, plus extra for dusting
250 ml (1 cup) lemonade
pinch of salt flakes
600 ml thickened cream
2 tablespoons milk
1½ tablespoons icing sugar,
   sifted, plus extra for dusting
315 g (1 cup) raspberry jam

PANTRY STAPLES	SHOPPING LIST
Butter	Lemonade
Icing sugar	
Milk	
Raspberry jam	
Salt	
Self-raising flour	
Thickened cream	

Preheat the oven to 200°C. Grease a 30 cm x 20 cm baking tin and line with baking paper, cutting into the corners to fit and extending the paper by 5 cm on each side (this makes it easier to lift the cake out).

Place the flour, lemonade, salt and 250 ml (1 cup) of cream in a large bowl and carefully mix with a butter knife until a soft dough forms. Tip out onto a lightly floured surface and gently bring the dough together. Don't over-knead or the scone cake will be tough. Carefully transfer to the prepared tin and press out to the edges. Brush the top with the milk and bake for 25–30 minutes until the cake is golden and a skewer inserted in the centre comes out clean. Cool in the tin for 5 minutes, then carefully lift out the cake and cool for a further 10 minutes on a wire rack.

Meanwhile, combine the icing sugar and the remaining cream in a bowl and whip to soft peaks.

Carefully cut the scone in half horizontally. Place the scone base on a cake stand or platter and smear over the jam, then top with dollops of whipped cream. Cover with the scone top, then dust with the extra icing sugar and serve.

RHUBARB AND HAZELNUT UPSIDE-DOWN CAKE

I love the tart, sweet flavour of rhubarb and hazelnuts are the perfect addition for a delicious upside-down cake. The most appealing thing about this recipe is the cake batter. No electric mixer is required, no gradual adding of ingredients – just place it all in a bowl and mix! Easy baking – now that's what I love.

SERVES: 8   PREP: 20 MINUTES   COOK: 1 HOUR 15 MINUTES

200 g unsalted butter, melted, plus extra for greasing
2 bunches of rhubarb (about 500 g), trimmed
grated zest and juice of 1 orange
285 g (1 ¼ cups) caster sugar
6 egg whites
175 g (1 ¾ cups) hazelnut meal (or almond or walnut meal)
75 g (½ cup) plain flour
1 ½ teaspoons vanilla extract
pinch of salt flakes
double cream, to serve

PANTRY STAPLES
Caster sugar
Eggs
Nut meal
Plain flour
Salt
Unsalted butter
Vanilla extract

SHOPPING LIST
Double cream
Orange
Rhubarb

Preheat the oven to 160°C. Grease the base and side of a 23 cm springform cake tin, line with baking paper and wrap the outside with foil to prevent leaking. Line a baking tray with baking paper and place the cake tin on top (this is just for extra insurance, in case any juices from the cake leak).

Trim and cut the rhubarb to cover the base of the tin, stacking if necessary to fill the gaps and use all the rhubarb. Pour on the orange juice, evenly scatter over 3 tablespoons of sugar and bake for 25 minutes until the rhubarb has collapsed a little and softened. Cool for 10 minutes.

Combine the remaining sugar with the butter, egg whites, nut meal, flour, vanilla, orange zest and salt in a bowl and mix with a wooden spoon to form a smooth batter. Pour over the rhubarb and return to the oven to bake for 45–50 minutes until a skewer inserted in the centre of the cake comes out clean. Stand in the tin for 15 minutes to cool slightly. Remove the collar of the tin, then place a plate on top of the cake and flip upside down. Carefully remove the base and baking paper. Serve the cake warm or at room temperature with a dollop of cream.

BAKED CITRUS CHEESECAKE

I wasn't really a fan of cheesecake until I tried the most delectable Basque version in San Sebastian. I went back to the same pintxos bar three times to get my daily dose, I loved it that much. I've been thinking about it ever since (as you do) and have recreated it here. It's not identical because the original doesn't have a biscuit base, but I like a layer of biscuit for texture and a bit of citrus for zing. The creamy, velvety centre is almost on par with the original. Enjoy! I know you will.

SERVES: 8   PREP: 20 MINUTES, PLUS OVERNIGHT CHILLING   COOK: 1 HOUR 30 MINUTES

80 g unsalted butter, melted,
   plus extra for greasing
180 g plain digestive biscuits
1 kg cream cheese, brought to
   room temperature for 1 hour
   before baking (see Note)
330 g (1 ½ cups) caster sugar
finely grated zest of 1 orange
finely grated zest of 1 lemon
5 eggs
375 ml (1 ½ cups) thickened cream
3 tablespoons plain flour, sifted
icing sugar, for dusting

Preheat the oven to 180°C.

Grease and line the base and side of a 20 cm springform cake tin with baking paper, making sure the paper extends 3 cm above the rim. Place on a baking tray and set aside until required.

Place the biscuits in a food processor and whiz until a crumb forms. Add the melted butter and pulse again until the mixture resembles wet sand. (Alternatively, place the biscuits in a zip-lock bag, break them up using a meat mallet or rolling pin and transfer them to a bowl before mixing in the butter.) Pour into the tin and press the biscuit mixture down firmly to form a compact, even layer.

Place the cream cheese, sugar and orange and lemon zests in the cleaned bowl of the food processor and blitz until smooth and creamy. Add the eggs one at a time, ensuring each egg has been incorporated before adding the next. Add the cream and flour and whiz until smooth and combined.

Pour the cream cheese mixture over the biscuit base, smooth the top with a spatula and place in the oven on the baking tray. Bake for 45 minutes until beginning to brown on top. Reduce the temperature to 150°C and bake for a further 35–45 minutes until the top is golden in colour with a slight wobble. Turn off the oven and let the cheesecake cool completely in the oven for 3–4 hours. Transfer to the fridge to chill overnight.

Serve the chilled cheesecake straight from the fridge, dusted with the icing sugar.

PANTRY STAPLES

Caster sugar
Eggs
Icing sugar
Lemon
Plain flour
Thickened cream
Unsalted butter

SHOPPING LIST

Cream cheese
Digestive biscuits
Orange

* It's crucial to bring the cream cheese to room temperature before baking to ensure there are no lumps. Simply remove from the fridge 1 hour before baking.

SELF-SAUCING CHOCOLATE PUDDING WITH BURNT MERINGUE CRUST

This is a real chocolate lover's dream: a gooey, molten lava-like centre and a crunchy crust topped with a marshmallow cloud crown. Need I say more?

SERVES: 6   PREP: 20 MINUTES   COOK: 35 MINUTES

200 g butter, plus extra for greasing
200 g dark chocolate (70% cacao),
   roughly chopped
2 eggs
4 egg yolks
80 g (⅓ cup) caster sugar
50 g (⅓ cup) self-raising flour
pinch of salt flakes
3 tablespoons cocoa powder
250 ml (1 cup) just-boiled water

BURNT MERINGUE
4 egg whites
230 g (1 cup) caster sugar

Preheat the oven to 200°C. Grease a 1.5 litre baking dish with butter.

Combine the butter and chocolate in a heatproof bowl and place over a saucepan of just-simmering water (don't let the bowl touch the water), stirring occasionally with a metal spoon until melted and smooth. Cool for 10 minutes. Keep the simmering water for the burnt meringue.

Place the eggs, egg yolks and 2 tablespoons of sugar in a bowl and lightly whisk until the sugar dissolves. Add to the melted chocolate mixture and stir with a metal spoon to combine. Add the flour, salt and 1½ tablespoons of cocoa and whisk to a smooth batter. Pour into the prepared dish.

Combine the remaining cocoa powder and sugar and scatter evenly over the pudding batter, then carefully pour over the boiling water. Bake for 20–25 minutes until the pudding is slightly firm on top and gooey in the centre.

Meanwhile, for the burnt meringue, place the egg whites and sugar in a heatproof bowl of an electric mixer and set over the saucepan of simmering water. Whisk constantly for 8–10 minutes until the sugar dissolves and the mixture becomes thick and glossy. (The temperature of the meringue should reach 72°C on a sugar thermometer.) Now, using your electric mixer fitted with the whisk attachment, whisk the meringue on high speed for 10 minutes until stiff, glossy and cooled.

Spoon dollops of the meringue over the pudding, swirl with the back of a spoon and use a blowtorch to caramelise. Serve immediately.

 To simplify, skip the meringue and serve the pudding with ice cream – it's just as delicious. Or you could scatter over a few store-bought marshmallows in the last 5 minutes of cooking and let them melt in the oven.

PANTRY STAPLES
Butter
Caster sugar
Cocoa powder
Dark chocolate
Eggs
Salt
Self-raising flour

CONVERSION CHARTS

Measuring cups and spoons may vary slightly from one country to another, but the difference is generally not enough to affect a recipe. All cup and spoon measures are level.

One Australian metric measuring cup holds 250 ml (8 fl oz), one Australian tablespoon holds 20 ml (4 teaspoons) and one Australian metric teaspoon holds 5 ml. North America, New Zealand and the UK use a 15 ml (3 teaspoon) tablespoon.

LENGTH

METRIC	IMPERIAL
3 mm	⅛ inch
6 mm	¼ inch
1 cm	½ inch
2.5 cm	1 inch
5 cm	2 inches
18 cm	7 inches
20 cm	8 inches
23 cm	9 inches
25 cm	10 inches
30 cm	12 inches

LIQUID MEASURES

ONE AMERICAN PINT	ONE IMPERIAL PINT
500 ml (16 fl oz)	600 ml (20 fl oz)

CUP	METRIC	IMPERIAL
⅛ cup	30 ml	1 fl oz
¼ cup	60 ml	2 fl oz
⅓ cup	80 ml	2½ fl oz
½ cup	125 ml	4 fl oz
⅔ cup	160 ml	5 fl oz
¾ cup	180 ml	6 fl oz
1 cup	250 ml	8 fl oz
2 cups	500 ml	16 fl oz
2¼ cups	560 ml	20 fl oz
4 cups	1 litre	32 fl oz

DRY MEASURES

The most accurate way to measure dry ingredients is to weigh them. However, if using a cup, add the ingredient loosely to the cup and level with a knife; don't compact the ingredient unless the recipe requests 'firmly packed'.

METRIC	IMPERIAL
15 g	½ oz
30 g	1 oz
60 g	2 oz
125 g	4 oz (¼ lb)
185 g	6 oz
250 g	8 oz (½ lb)
375 g	12 oz (¾ lb)
500 g	16 oz (1 lb)
1 kg	32 oz (2 lb)

OVEN TEMPERATURES

CELSIUS	FAHRENHEIT
100°C	200°F
120°C	250°F
150°C	300°F
160°C	325°F
180°C	350°F
200°C	400°F
220°C	425°F

CELSIUS	GAS MARK
110°C	¼
130°C	½
140°C	1
150°C	2
170°C	3
180°C	4
190°C	5
200°C	6
220°C	7
230°C	8
240°C	9
250°C	10

THANKS

There are many fingerprints on the pages of this delicious cookbook, not just mine. This book would not exist without the support, passion and incredible hard work of the A-team below. You are all exceptional and I thank you from the bottom of my heart for bringing this beautiful book to life.

First, to the wonderful Plum team at Pan Macmillan. Mary Small, you are so much more than an extraordinarily passionate publisher! In the first cookbook we published together, I think I called you 'the fairy Godmother' – there's no other way to describe you. You've nurtured, encouraged and then made all of my slightly annoying ideas not only come to life, but work so brilliantly.

Clare Marshall, we worked together the closest on this book and I wouldn't have it any other way. You're simply one of the most patient, meticulous and thoughtful people I've ever worked with. I can't thank you enough for all your words of wisdom, being my sounding board and keeping me in line with the dreaded deadlines. Did I mention how patient I think you are? Haha.

Photographer extraordinaire, Jeremy Simons, it's been an absolute pleasure working with you on this project. I adore every single photo in the book. You just make everything look extra yummy through the lens! It was also great to have your adorable dog, Chefo, assisting us on set – he was invaluable to the team.

Oh, Vanessa Austin! We've been working together for three years now; you are the trendiest stylist I know. Thank you for being so tolerant of my many last-minute changes to the dishes, for making my food shine, and for occasionally letting me steal some of your wardrobe for the perfect shot. You have an incredible eye for detail.

Warren Mendes (Waz), you're an absolute dream to work with. Two weeks of hardcore cooking with you for the book shoot was like child's play. Always making me laugh and always so accurate in recreating my dishes (except the chicken and pea bake, leave that one to me!), there's a reason why you have me and Matt Preston fighting over you – we just love your work, matey!

A huge thanks to Megan Johnston, the queen of fine-toothcomb editing – my recipes are always in safe hands with you. To the always-imaginative designer, Kirby Armstrong, for your beautiful layouts, and to darling Charlotte Ree – for not only ensuring that my book gets out into the world and into the hands of the home cook, but also for popping by while shooting, rolling up your sleeves and effortlessly making a quick batch of my tiramisu. You nailed it!

To Sam Coutts, cheers for dropping everything to help me test some of my recipes when you knew my deadline was approaching. You're like a Speedy Gonzalez.

My dear friend Amy Russo, I'm always so amazed at how you can transform my clumsy words into magical ones when you know it's hard for me to describe my sheer love of food! To Maddy Scott, you joined us on your work experience week and boy did you amaze us with your incredible passion to learn about cooking and food styling. Sorry that Waz made you do the washing up, occasionally.

Lisa and Caitlin Sullivan, my right-hand women. Ten years of working together has gone by so quickly. Thank you for always believing in me and making my dreams come true!

To my family, what on earth would I do without you? I am so lucky to have you. I would not be able to follow any of these dreams without the encouragement, tireless support and love you show me every single day.

Last, but certainly not least, a HUGE thanks to you, the reader! It's your constant support and belief in my recipes that allows me to write cookbooks and do what I love most … cook for you.

Justine
ox

INDEX

ABOUT JUSTINE

Justine Schofield has made a career of inspiring home cooks around the country, from
her television debut on the first series of *MasterChef Australia* to her long-running role as host of
Channel Ten's *Everyday Gourmet* – now in its ninth season. Justine runs a boutique catering company
and is the author of the bestselling cookbooks *Dinner with Justine* (2016) and *Simple Every Day* (2017).
Justine lives in Sydney.

justineschofield.com.au

A PLUM BOOK

First published in 2019 by
Pan Macmillan Australia Pty Limited
Level 25, 1 Market Street,
Sydney, NSW 2000, Australia

Level 3, 112 Wellington Parade,
East Melbourne, VIC 3002, Australia

Design by Kirby Armstrong
Edited by Megan Johnston
Index by Helena Holmgren
Photography by Jeremy Simons
Prop and food styling by Vanessa Austin
Food preparation by Warren Mendes and Justine Schofield
Typeset by Kirby Jones
Colour reproduction by Splitting Image Colour Studio
Printed and bound in China by 1010 Printing International Limited

A CIP catalogue record for this book is available from the National Library of Australia.

10 9 8 7 6 5 4 3 2 1